THE MEMOIRS OF
JACK FAIRFAX-BLAKEBOROUGH
O.B.E., M.C.

"J.F-B"

EDITED BY

Noel Fairfax-Blakeborough

J. A. ALLEN
LONDON & NEW YORK

ISBN 0-85131-269-1

Published in Great Britain in 1978 by
J. A. Allen & Company Limited,
1, Lower Grosvenor Place, Buckingham Palace Road,
London, SW1W 0EL
and in the United States of America by
Sporting Book Center, Inc.,
Canaan, N.Y. 12029

Printed in Great Britain by
REDWOOD BURN LIMITED
Trowbridge & Esher

CONTENTS

LIST OF ILLUSTRATIONS

PREFACE

by Noel Fairfax-Blakeborough

The countryfolk in lonely Westerdale, where my father lived, were convinced that he led an easy life. He was always ready for a chat and always had a good story to tell. He did not plough, reap or sow . . . he just sat and wrote.

For 30 years everyone in that North Yorkshire dale could count on a warm welcome at his 17th century home on the edge of the moor. Callers found him sitting at his desk or in an easy chair, pen in hand, papers on his knee. They thought what a simple job he had. But very few men packed more into a lifetime — and his spanned 93 full years — or gave more enjoyment, entertainment and information.

My father shared in many roles while playing his part in the Turf revolution. He was racehorse owner, trainer, amateur rider, judge, racecourse official, historian, racing journalist and columnist. Work recognised by his O.B.E. award.

He wrote 112 books and thousands of columns for scores of newspapers. Latterly writing was his life — his strength. He was a humorist, novelist, commentator, descriptive writer and serious historian.

Most of my father's actual writing was accomplished in the quiet that follows darkness. He regularly worked until midnight and after, but before his desk light was switched off he faithfully recorded the experiences of each day in his diary. He was meticulous about this, and rewrote in precis form a diary captured by the Germans during the First World War.

My father was a devoted family man — but this narrative is

not about his private life. Enough that my mother and father were a completely happy couple, and he certainly could not have achieved success as an author had she not been his shield against interruption, provider of food whatever the unlikely hour — and his loving, constant and absolutely understanding partner. My mother fashioned an unselfish life to suit the demands of a writer enthralled with his work. She did so without murmur of complaint or suggestion of loneliness, indeed acting all the while with encouragement and enthusiastic support. An accomplished artist, she illustrated a number of my father's books and so played a vital part in his success.

My father's diaries are a major source for this book, which is autobiographical in that all the events recorded here were done so by my father. My own part in the preparation of his manuscript for publication has been to edit and generally tidy up his text. To this I have also added his favourite stories as told to me, and drawn on conversations that we had over the years about racing, racecourse personalities and horses. Also I have included detail from material my father left among his papers.

My father died on January 1, 1976. He had been busy at his typewriter until a few hours before his death, and his diary was almost up-to-date. My greatest difficulty has been deciding what to omit. Every word is my father's, and I only hope that the following pages catch some reflection of all the happiness, fun and experience that were packed into his 93 years.

NOEL FAIRFAX-BLAKEBOROUGH

It is said that all those who go racing are rogues and vagabonds. That may not be true. But it is true that all rogues and vagabonds go racing.

SIR ABE BAILEY

If I were to begin my life again, I would go to the turf for friends. They seem to me to be the only people who really hold close together. It may be that each knows something that might hang the other — but the effect is altogether delightful.

LADY ASHBURTON

CHAPTER ONE

TO HORSE

I was born at Guisborough in Yorkshire on January 16, 1883. My father was an author and playwright and on his side I am descended from the Fairfax family. The Fairfaxes, together with the Duke of Buckingham – who married a Fairfax – played a large part in the foundation of the breed of the thoroughbred, the racehorse of today. Right down the ages the Fairfax family have been horsemen, cavalrymen, horse-lovers and horse-breeders and until his death my kinsman, Col. Brian Fairfax had the Blink Bonny stud at Malton.

I was horse mad almost as soon as I could walk and, at the age of seven, I can remember a cousin and myself taking off our little braces, using them as bridles on ponies we caught in a field near Redcar and having a race meeting there on our own.

At Guisborough there was a horse-dealer, horse-breaker, and fine horseman called John Walton. Almost daily he brought in long reins the horses he was "making", to lunge and figure-of-eight on the church-green opposite the house – built by my great-grandfather – in which I was born. When I was about eight years old I waited for his arrival and always ran out to join him. Often he put me up on young horses and so began my first, most valuable lessons in horsemanship. I could not have had a better, more experienced, or more candid tutor.

"Keep those hands and heels down."

"Don't sit like a cat on a darning-needle, or a sack of corn."

"Never jag a horse in the mouth."

"Treat your reins as though they were silk and would snap if you jerked at them, or tried to hold on to them."

I can hear it all now after ninety-two years have passed! John Walton and his sons did more for horse-breeding and horsemanship than anyone will ever know and the pleasure he gave me, I have remembered all through my life. I have always been grateful to him for taking so much trouble with a little boy who must have been rather a nuisance. Truly, it is said: "Make a child happy today and you make him happy 20 years hence." I think love of horses and riding must have been born in me. John Walton unconsciously helped to shape and found my long sporting career.

When my elder brother Ric and I became school age father sent us to the village school at Hutton Lowcross. He made this choice because the schoolmaster was a Cambridge graduate, and by far the most educated teacher in the area. Nevertheless this meant that when only five years old I had to walk the two miles to school from Guisborough whatever the weather. Ric was with me, of course, but he was a couple of years older and had longer legs. We had sandwiches for our lunches and in the evening walked home again. These daily treks were made easier by Ric who had a great knowledge of the birds that nested in the hedgerows, and was also quick to spot a stoat or a young leveret dashing for cover. Ric and I became very close and it was the heart-break of my life when he was killed in a shooting accident while in his teens. The shotgun fired accidentally as he climbed through a hedge while after rabbits.

William Winn was associated with the opening of another chapter in my varied sporting career. For it was from his Ayton Hall in 1891 that I set out on my first day's hunting. The fixture was a mile or so away from Cliffe Ridge. Mr. Winn provided champagne for all comers. Although only eight years old I was given a sip of champagne and I thought then — and I have never altered my opinion — that the white wine of France is a very over-rated drink though I have many times since welcomed a glass or two as a pick-me-up at eleven o'clock in the morning.

I think it was Mr. Walton who pointed me out to Mr.

Winn. Possibly he told him that he had been putting me up on some of the horses he was breaking, that I was very keen, and that he had been giving me some instructions in riding.

I was ten years old and went on foot from Guisborough to Redcar on Whit Monday 1893 for my first day's racing. And, if I remember rightly, there was no charge for those who watched racing "outside". If there was gate money it was only a copper or two.

Like Bob Colling, who was riding at the meeting, I was born within a few miles of the Redcar course, so it was my home meeting and had a particular interest for me from the time that I first became keen on horses and sport. My mother had told me of attending Redcar races when they were held on the sands. Indeed, the meeting continued to be on the sea shore until 1873, when the present racecourse was developed.

I think, apart from a longing to see thoroughbreds in action, the main incentive for visiting Redcar that day was that the Rt. Hon. James Lowther — who lived at Witton Castle, and was a very active member of the Jockey Club as well as one of the Stewards and main supporters of Redcar races — had told my father that he was certain to win the big race with First Consul. So he did, with Jim Fagan riding, and I had a shilling on the winner. This "big" race, by the way, was the Saltburn Handicap which was worth £200 and the total prize money for the two days was £1,377.

On the second day First Consul was saddled successfully again, winning the Langbaurgh Plate carrying 11st 3lb which included a 10lb penalty. I backed the horse again and as Jim Fagan at once became a hero in my eyes, I had another shilling on his mount in the next race. Again he won — this time on Mark Macgregor at 3-1. Feeling myself a Rothschild but remembering Yorkshireman's caution, I kept my winnings in my pocket and had no more bets.

About the worst thing that could happen to a youth was to have three bets and back three winners on his first trip racing. Fortunately, however, I was not bitten by the gambling bug, and since the end of the First World War I have had only one bet. Simply because Royal Palace was owned by my old friend Jim Joel, I successfully wagered £100 to £500 over the brilliant colt's Derby triumph. Wagering never gave me what is termed "an interest" but rather detracted from the pleasure of racing. It has always been the horses, and all that is best in the sport, which has appealed to me rather than trying to find winners and to get a point above the odds.

During my long Turf career I have seen a lot of clever, astute, well-informed backers come and go. Some of them won and lost fortunes and eventually faded out, disappearing owing the ring money and were barred from attending race meetings. I knew one well-known Yorkshireman, on "the black list" because he had not settled his bookmaker's account, who continued to go racing disguised with a false moustache and spectacles.

As I have said, I was only ten years old and Jim Fagan and Bob Colling became idols. I longed to emulate them. They were both about ten years older than myself but a decade later both became my close friends.

Jim and Bob were both riding for William I'Anson's then all conquering Highfield Stables at Malton — where Bill Elsey now trains. Fagan was very successful as a jockey and won six Gimcrack Stakes between 1885 and 1897. He also won an Ebor Handicap (1885) Cumberland Plates (1877 and 1886), Northumberland Plates (1884 and 1896), Chester Cups (1892 and 1893) and many other important events for I'Anson. When he gave up riding he bought and modernised the Grove House Yard at Malton. He was fairly well off but sank most of his capital in buying and improving his house and stables. Then he got a number of patrons who did not pay their training fees and practically ruined him. He had to sell Grove House for £2,500 — less than half the sum that he had paid for the property. I was then able to be of some little assistance and he received an allowance from the Bentinck Memorial Fund, founded to help jockeys and trainers who fall on evil days, until he died in 1932.

When Bob Colling gave up riding he started farming at Habton, but eventually started as a trainer in 1899 at Spigot Lodge, Middleham. He never wished to leave Spigot Lodge and Yorkshire, but his main patron wanted to have his horses in the South, so Bob moved to Waterwitch House, Newmarket during the First World War. One of the last Northern race meetings he attended was Redcar, when we talked over old times, and discussed my first day's racing there. He recalled that his own first experience of racing was also at Redcar, his father farming within a mile of the course. He was originally intended for the church but all his forbears had been horsey and hunting men. The saddle appealed to him more than the cassock and he was apprenticed to Bob Armstrong at Penrith.

Jimmy Lowther made Wilton Castle a great sporting centre, farming and breeding Cleveland Bay horses on a large scale. Although not a hunting man himself, Jimmy was a great supporter of the Cleveland Hunt. He was also keen on coursing and there were always good foxes and stout hares on his estate. The Cleveland Coursing Club had one or two attractive meetings there every year and it was at Wilton that I had my first experience of the sport, but though I have always admired the speed, symmetry and turning powers of the greyhound, coursing has never appealed to me. At the time of the Wilton meetings there were a great many people in Cleveland and on Teesside who kept greyhounds and were members of various local coursing clubs which then existed. Catterick had a very strong club and eighty years ago Redcar also had a popular one with headquarters at The Jolly Sailor, kept by George Fall. I remember attending a coursing dinner there at which we sat packed like herrings in a box because there was no room big enough for such an occasion. Time after time we sang the chorus of a local song . . . .

Fill the bowl, fill it flowing, since life glides apace,
And health be the toast to the great coursing race!
To the greyhound's winged speed, wheresoe'er it abounds,
Till time calls away to the field, park and downs.

Fill the bowl they constantly did. It was some time before I recovered from that dinner. I never attended another! Most of my coursing experience afterwards was in private and on the property of Frank Dobson, at Dromonby, near Stokesley. Frank was a great admirer of greyhounds and on many occasions we went out for a course with two or three from his kennel. This I found interesting, for there was neither the slaughter, the artificiality, crowd and noise of a public coursing meeting. One of Frank's daughters married Ossy Casebourne, who was then training at Middleham.

Ossy Casebourne, his brothers Vernon and Creswell and I, were all at the same school together. Years later, Cres, with the late Jack French, was mainly responsible for starting the Cleveland Park greyhound track. Against my will, Cres got me to act as judge there for 1928, the first year of its existence. Often I had been in the judge's box at some Northern horse race meeting miles away and was far too mentally exhausted and physically tired to adjudicate in the evening on the greyhound track. I found the spectators quite a different class to those who supported horse racing. At Cleveland Park there were boos and yells of "Put your bloody spectacles on," "Give a fair decision," "Get another judge," when a favourite was beaten. Quite frankly I hated every minute of it, and when my year's contract was up I retired. The directors presented me with a free pass to the course and grandstand. I see it is dated 1929. I have never used it, and have never been on any other greyhound track since. At Cleveland Park Syd Morton of Middlesbrough was the official vet. He and I were old friends both of the hunting field and the old Cleveland Polo Club, which had a ground just outside Nunthorpe station. Syd Morton, a nice lightweight, and a good horseman, was one of the mainstays. Others were land agency pupils with Jock Clarke at Guisborough, including Hubert Goodman, who later took the name of Dorington and Mastered the Bilsdale Hounds.

Wherever there was sport there one found Syd Morton. He was at most Northern race meetings, a follower of the Cleveland

Hunt, and everywhere in Cleveland and Teesside where horsemen and horses were brought together. I know he had much more interest in horses than greyhounds and didn't think much of greyhound racing as a sport. Personally, I always thought there was a lot more fun and less artificiality in whippet racing than in greyhound racing. If only whippet fans had not been so noisy and if there had not been so much "cooking" of races.

Quite near my old home at Grove House, Norton, there was a whippet racing track at Belle Vue. Once this had been a gentleman's residence. There was a long carriage-drive up to the house and there was stabling for carriage-horses, and the remains of what had been spacious gardens. But in the 1930's Belle Vue had deteriorated. Only the gateway to the drive told us of past glories. The house, used as a club, was in an unpainted, uncared for condition. The gardens were a waste, and two or three nights a week there were dog races. Lots of people in Norton, Stockton and Thornaby kept whippets, and every day one saw them being trained in the Norton-road recreation ground. At that time there were scores of whippet tracks in South Durham. The stakes were quite small and the bookmakers who attended were very cautious about taking bets of any amount over £1.

The Durham pitmen were famed both for their whippets and their Bedlington terriers. There was careful handicapping of dogs and great art in handling and throwing them forward so that they landed on their feet when the starter fired his pistol. I fancy greyhound racing killed the sport with whippets, which are now rarely seen on Teesside. A story is told of a Stockton vicar remonstrating with a man whose children had neither boots nor stockings but whose whippets wore beautiful warm clothing. The parson suggested that it would be much better for the family if the man kept a pig instead of whippets. The reply was: "A bonny feeal I should look takking a pig ti Bell Vue ti race!"

CHAPTER TWO

EARLY DAYS

At school I got no prizes, was never top of a form, never did a sum right or learned the first thing about Euclid, science or chemistry. The masters must have been sorely tried. Yet I have happy memories of my days at Hutton Lowcross and at Stockton Grammar School. My mother and father moved to a house in Trent Street, Norton-On-Tees, when I left the village preparatory school so I became a pupil at Stockton Grammar School — a mile away from this new home.

When I left school my father was anxious that I should become a stock and share broker and had me articled to an investment expert in Middlesbrough. Father had spent an often precarious life from a financial viewpoint, filling the roles of author, playwright and actor. He reasoned that the world of the Stock Exchange would be far more secure — but after just six months in the "bull" and "bear" office the pull of the horse became too strong for me.

I was already interested in journalism, so decided that this profession was the one most likely to allow me to open the stable door as it were. I was lucky. I joined a conservative evening newspaper which had just been started on Teesside in opposition to *The North Eastern Daily Gazette*.

The editor took me as a premium-paying pupil — tea boy and copy carrier. I was, however, soon writing and sub-editing and gaining valuable experience. Unfortunately the newspaper folded, but the lessons I had learned enabled me to claim some expertise, and I made the most of this when I applied for a post on the *Gazette*. Again I was lucky and on July 6, 1900, I received a letter from John Kealey, General Manager of *The North Eastern Daily Gazette* at Middlesbrough: "I have pleasure in accepting your services as a reporter at a salary of thirty shillings per week to commence with, subject to one month's notice on either side." This was a really lucky break for a 17 year old boy. I happily joined the staff of the *Gazette* and for a year or so wrote on racing and hunting and three of us got out the *Sports Gazette* every Saturday night.

I started at 9 a.m. and on Saturday we had tea brought into the office and had a nine-hour stint. In those days there were only two sub-editors on the paper so we younger birds had to take a turn at sub-editing. I think on Saturday evenings I was everything. I contributed a racing and hunting article of one or two columns; I sub-edited hundreds of telegrams which were dropping into a box at the rate of two every five minutes; I took reports over the telephone and, occasionally, racing results. We had a hectic few hours but it was great fun and valuable experience.

However, I hated office work and loved the country. I had gone to live at the Old Hall at Battersby in 1901 and occasionally rode into Middlesbrough and put up my horse in a loose-box at an hotel in Linthorpe Road quite near the *Gazette* office which was in Zetland-road.

In 1903 at the age of 20 I decided to branch out as a free-lance sporting writer. During the next few months I acquired sufficient regular racing and hunting literary work to justify my keeping two or three hunters and enjoying sport with the Cleveland, Bilsdale and Hurworth packs. I had a couple of horses stabled with John Megginson at Battersby and hunted three or four days a week. I became very friendly with Canon Kyle, of Carlton-in-Cleveland, who hunted occasionally with the Cleveland and Hurworth, and with his brother-in-law, Fred Wilson Horsfall, afterwards Master of the Bilsdale Hunt. That friendship became very real and deepened as the years passed, ending only with the death of those two lovable personalities. It was Horsfall and Sir Alfred Pease who were mainly responsible for my life-long connection with Cleveland Bay horses and the Cleveland Bay Horse Society. Horsfall had a big stud of Clevelands at Potto, the ace being that great mare Lady Salton.

In 1903 David Smallwood and I were judges at the horse races then held in the Didderhow field at Castleton. Little did I think that 20 years later I should be a licensed Turf judge. Before the Castleton races the judges lunched with the officials at the nearby Buck Inn — now two private houses.

David Smallwood was a horse-dealer, kept The Angel Inn at Whitby, and had been Master of the defunct Eskdale Hounds. He was a jovial character. I had first met him when he entertained Henry Selby Lowndes, Fred Horsfall, myself and two or three others at his Whitby pub. He put-up us, our horses and the Bilsdale hounds for a couple of nights without charge when we went to hunt what had been the Eskdale country. Selby Lowndes — afterwards long Master of the East Kent — was at that time Master of the Bilsdale and had as his whipper-in John Boyes, of Castleton. Lowndes was a great beer drinker. David Smallwood preferred whisky and frankly admitted that it had cost him a fortune to paint his nose the colour it was. He was a great sportsman and had as his right hand man Bert Wren, who afterwards had a horse dealing business at Pickering. I fancy David was mainly responsible for arranging a National Hunt race meeting they had a Grinkle Park for a year or two.

The Castleton horse races were great fun and I can still remember how well a little lad called Marsay — whose father had the inn at Moorsholm — rode both on the flat and over hurdles on a mare called Woodland's Lass. The event was on Whit Monday, June 1, 1903 and the charge for admission was sixpence. The Rosedale Brass Band played, no betting was allowed, and the judge's decisions were final. There was a handicap trotting race first, then a flat race of one-and-a-half miles, with £3 for the winner and £1 for the second. This was the "big race" and was won by Woodland's Lass. Then came a pony race followed by a hurdle race of one-and-a-half miles, which I think T. Swales of Yarm, won. He had a butcher's business and also dealt in horses. He used to hunt with the Hurworth, and was a good light-weight horseman. There was as much excitement and interest in those little Castleton races as though they had been the Derby and Grand National rolled into one. No one rode in racing colours and there were no number-cloths, but the whole afternoon was marked by a truly sporting atmosphere, very different to the commercial aspect of horse racing in these days.

At this period, in my early twenties, I usually stayed for York races with Bob Robson, who had a charming estate at Farnham, near Knaresborough, on which he trained a number of horses of his own and all Compton Vyner's jumpers. The first time I stayed with Robson both the famous John Porter and Bob Colling were among the guests. For years Bob Robson and Colling shared a shoot and often Robson invited both the then Middleham trainer and myself to hunt with the York and Ainsty. Robson always lived above his means. He gambled far too heavily and entertained far too lavishly. Only the best was good enough for his guests. When there was a shortage of ready money — as there often was — Robson would ring up a butcher or cattle-dealer to come immediately to buy half a dozen of the cattle, or a score of sheep from his park. He was a lovable character, a very good amateur rider, and a real friend. Above all he was a horse lover, and an extremely shrewd and clever trainer.

There is little wonder that a youth like myself, just setting out on a Turf career, hero worshipped Porter. He trained the winners of seven Derbys, six St. Legers, three Oaks and five Two Thousand Guineas. His Derby winners included three Triple Crown heroes: Ormonde (1886) Common (1891) and Flying Fox (1899). Before retiring in 1905 Porter saddled the winners of more than 1,000 races worth over £720,000 in stake money — a fantastic sum in those days. That record certainly justified hero worship, but a more modest man than John Porter I have never met. This is surely a characteristic of the really great men in every profession. Sir Cecil Boyd-Rochfort was just the same, despite all his success — 13 classic winners and victories in a total of 1,169 races worth more than £1,600,000. He trained for Kings and Queens of England from 1943 until he retired in 1968. Cecil never threw his weight about despite his intimacy with Royal patrons and others of high degree. How different the attitudes of these two grand men to the cockiness of some trainers after they have won a few minor races these days.

Yet Porter was full of admiration for the hard working conscientious Northern trainers. "I always said that I could train a good horse by the side of the road. It is the bad and bad-legged beggars which require so much attention. North-country trainers can win races with them when they have been sold at Newmarket as useless" he once told me.

John Porter also told me some interesting things about the great mare La Fleche, with which he had won the 1892 St. Leger and Oaks. She was second in the Derby and her trainer thought that she would have won easily had not F. Barrett ridden a far-too-confident race. According to Porter, Sir Tatton Sykes was furious with his wife paying 12,600 guineas for La Fleche at the 1896 Sales after the death of the owner Baron Rirsch. Sir Tatton did not consider the horse was worth anything like that but Lady Sykes was determined to have her and went on bidding until the figure was the highest every paid for a brood mare at public auction. Despite the fact that she was an irregular breeder, her yearlings brought 17,900 guineas to the Sledmere Stud so she probably paid her way, just.

Porter knew that I had ambitions to become a trainer, and his advice was: "Don't start with patrons who want to be clever and won't run their horses straight. They are the sort who prefer their horses in little stables and with beginners, who don't pay their bills, and who get trainers into trouble." It is truer on the Turf than in any other walk of like, that a man is judged by the company he keeps. If a young man associates with the "clever" brigade and the riff-raff of racing, he descends to their level in the estimation of others. John Porter was a delightful man and a very sound counsellor.

John Osborne, the famous Middleham trainer was another great friend and mentor in my early racing days. I was often at his splendid Brecongil stables from 1903 until his death at the age of 89 in 1922. John trained the famous mare Lily Agnes, the dam of Ormonde, Orme, Sceptre and Flying Fox. Lily Agnes was a very good race mare herself, and won 21 races including the Northumberland Plate and Doncaster Cup in 1874 and the Ebor Handicap the following year.

I also learned from John Osborne a great deal about stable management and the preparation of horses before they raced. For several years I saddled his runners before they ran. I can hear him saying: "Keep your hand firm on the top of the saddle. I like the saddle well forward and hate any shouting or fuss to unsettle horses when they are being saddled."

I never heard John use a swear word. I never heard him tell a dirty story. He did not smoke, and was a most abstemious man. Dressed more like a Nonconformist parson than a trainer, he didn't like starched collars, or wearing neckties. He went to bed early, rarely had a bet, and when he did it was a very modest one. Throughout his long life he was never associated with anything crooked on the Turf and, though he had forgotten more about racing, bloodstock, training and riding than most of us ever knew, he never criticised, offered an opinion or advice, except when asked. Then, diffidence and modesty characterised all he said. At home he was more a country farmer than a distinguished ex-jockey and trainer, and we had many an interesting chat in his comfortable Victorian sitting-room.

We were often joined by Dobson Peacock who, with his sons Matt and Harry, was very fond of John. They all had great respect and affection for him and Matt and Harry were more like sons to him in his last years.

I will never forget Osborne's and Peacock's kindness in making the awkward journey to see me when I was in bed at

Carlton-in-Cleveland vicarage in 1903 after a bad riding accident which the Press had magnified into a broken back. Canon Kyle had taken me out one day to his stables at Handley Cross. There we saw one of his horses, a steeplechaser which had always bolted and run himself to a standstill. A chestnut who stood over 17 hands and was a hard puller, he could buck like a wild west bronco and had been having too much corn and too little work. I heard all about his character but, with the conceit and self-assurance of youth, I asked to be allowed to have a ride on him with a view to purchase. I felt he only wanted someone on his back who wasn't nervous and who would "kid" to him. We saddled him, the parson gave me a leg up and I said I would ride him up the steep hill leading to Raisdale and Bilsdale.

In the middle of Carlton Village some boys were trundling iron hoops and one of these flew into the hind legs of my mount. He took his bit between his teeth and bolted. I thought climbing Carlton Bank would tire and steady him, but before reaching its foot we had to pass the vicarage where he had previously been stabled. Whipping round suddenly there he jumped the big, spiked iron gates, pecked on landing and came down. I was hurled, in a circus somersault, with such force against a gatepost that I thought my spine was broken. So it was, but only the end of it, the coccyx, where the tail of human being ends. I lay for some days in great pain, hardly able to move. Although I soon recovered the crushing fall had knocked some of the conceit and cockiness out of me.

How they got to out-of-the-way Carlton-in-Cleveland — nearest station a couple of miles away, and only about four trains a day — I don't know, but John Osborne and Dobson Peacock came to see me after being at Stockton Races. Canon and Mrs. Kyle made them very welcome and were particularly interested to meet John Osborne and to hear that in his jockey days he rode his first classic winner for a parson, the Rev. J. W. King who raced as "Mr. Launde", for whom his father trained. Not only did Osborne win the 1,000 Guineas for "Mr. Launde" but 20 years later he steered his horse Apology to win the 1874

Oaks, the St. Leger and the 1,000 Guineas. Three Classics in one season was too much for the parson's bishop who wrote him a letter of reproof. The Rev. King replied that his family had bred bloodstock for generations and that he could not see that his continuing the breed and testing their merits on racecourses constituted a scandal in the Church. John Osborne knew the letter by heart and said it concluded: "I desire to live the remainder of my days in peace and charity with all men and I resign my living, not from any consciousness of wrong, or fear of futile proceedings being taken against me in the ecclesiastical courts, but simply to avoid the scandal of such proceedings."

I fancy Canon Kyle drove Osborne and Peacock either to Picton or Northallerton to catch a train back to Leyburn. John Osborne said he felt he must come to see me to reassure me I would soon be well and riding again. He also had once had his coccyx broken when riding at Durham races. He considered the Durham course and those at Newcastle – when on the Town Moor – and Musselburgh were the most dangerous he ever rode on. In 1885 at Durham, his mount slipped and he was thrown against the rails. That the rails were broken where his back hit them, shows with what force he was thrown. He said there were no ambulances or ambulance men in those days and, as he lay on the ground, some of the crowd which gathered said: "His back is broken." Another said: "If his back's broken he can't move his legs." Then some of them began to pull his legs and decided his back was not broken. However his coccyx was. Lord Durham's bus took him to the Three Tuns Hotel in Durham where he lay for ten weeks.

I wasn't more than ten days on my back before I was able to leave Carlton vicarage at which I, and the stream of visitors to see me, must have been a great nuisance. I was never made to feel it was so. Soon I was again out four or five days a week with the Cleveland, Hurworth and Bilsdale packs, hunting all day and writing all night. I often went to Danby Hall, near Middleham, to stay with Simon Conyers Scrope, and whipped in to the hounds he had got together to hunt the moorland portion of the Bedale country. Conyers and his brother Stephen were two of my closest friends.

Conyers was almost entirely a hunting man – though he rode in point-to-points – while Stephen devoted his latter years to racing during the day and playing bridge at night. This was particularly the case after the bad accident he had when out hunting with the Bedale. His horse put a foot down in a rabbit-hole, came down, rolled over him and caused spinal injuries which kept him on his back for some years. He lay out all one frosty night after his fall – despite search parties seeking him with lanterns – was never able to ride again and was rarely free from pain. He turned his whole attention to racing and had a number of horses in training, one of the last of them being Snowcrest, who won 10 races and was strongly fancied for the Northumberland Plate in 1920.

Since the earliest days of the Turf the Scropes have been among the main supporters of racing in the North. They were Lords of Bolton, Masham and Upsall, Earls of Wiltes and vast landowners. It used to be said they could ride from Danby-on-Yore to Lincolnshire without ever being off their own land. But, after the Reformation, their adherence to the Catholic faith resulting in their losing titles and estates, and compelled them to run their horses in the names of friends. One of the many disabilities imposed on Catholics was that they were not allowed to own a horse worth more than £5. To be more correct, they were bound to sell any horse they had for that amount if demanded. This, of course, meant that they could not personally be identified with their racehorses. It is remarkable how hereditary has been the love of bloodstock and racing in the ancient family! This is so today with the descendants of Conyers and Stephen, Adrian Scrope having had a long association with Lord Derby's, and the Sledmere, studs.

Adrian, of course, married a sister of Sir Richard Sykes and for some years lived at Sledmere after an educational period with Harry Peacock when the latter was running the Spigot

Lodge stud at Middleham. For a time he acted as whipper-in when Sir Richard Sykes was Master of the East Middleton country.

The present head of the family at Danby-on-Yore, near Ripon, is Richard Scrope, who breeds blood horses. He married a sister of Lord Ellesmere and is a Steward at Northern race meetings. His son and mine were together at Ampleforth College, where Scrope was Master of the College Beagles. Simon Scrope as representative for a world-wide bloodstock agency is seen at every Northern fixture, and is one of the most respected and popular paddock personalities. His judgement is valued and he misses nothing as he critically watches the performance of horses, sizing-up their value and stud potential.

Simon Conyers Scrope — uncle of the three brothers just mentioned — was a bachelor. It was one of his life's ambitions to again have hounds in the old kennels at Danby and to hunt the hill part of the Bedale country. Unfortunately all his plans ended in disappointment.

Conyers engaged Jack Petts as kennel huntsman. He had been for some years huntsman in the Hurworth country during the long Mastership of William Forbes. The new pack consisted mainly of Welsh hounds from the Radnor and West Hereford. They proved unsteady and started sheep-worrying. I was out with them on their final day near Middleham when they failed to find a fox.Then they ran sheep, killed two and were there and then condemned. We had a very miserable dinner that night. There were four of us — our host, his brother Gervase, who hunted hounds, the Marquis of Exeter and myself. Our host wept in his distress that the desire of his life had to have such a miserable ending. He had signed the death warrant of the whole pack, and the execution was to be on the morrow. I don't think Conyers Scrope ever quite got over the blow.

In more recent times, W. E. Burrill, of Masham, formed another pack to hunt the West of Yore part of the Bedale country. He hunted hounds himself with Richard Scrope whipping in to him. I certainly had many happy days when visiting Conyers at Danby and Stephen when he lived at Duchy Court, Harrogate. Latterly half of Danby was covered in dust sheets. We dined in what had been the housekeeper's room and one faithful old butler looked after us without the aid of the two footmen who, before, had always been in attendance. The butler brought hot water to our bedrooms morning and night for hip-baths. I fancy in those days there was but one bathroom at Danby Hall, though I do not remember ever being in it. Richard Scrope has brought the historic and delightful old place up-to-date. He, by the way, has as his racing colours the *"azure a bend or"* (azure with gold belt) which 600 years ago was the object of an historic trial in the Herald's court of chivalry. In 1385 the Grosvenors – ancestors of the Dukes of Westminster and Devonshire – claimed the *"azure a bend or"* for their arms but failed as the Scropes proved their right to them as "the ablest tournyers of all their country", a distinction won by Sir William Scrope in a tournament in early Plantagenet times. Conyers Scrope told me once that the late Duke of Westminster wrote to his father for permission to name his famous horse, Bend Or, as did Cunliffe Lister to take title of Baron Masham, when he was raised to the peerage. By right Richard Scrope is the twentieth Earl of Wiltes, that title having been conferred to his ancestor by Richard II in 1397 "to him and his heirs male for ever." The first earl was Sir William Scrope, son of Lord Scrope of Bolton. It is truly stated in the volume *A Great Historic Peerage* that "the history of the Scropes is for some time the history of Yorkshire, indeed the North of England. Again and again there was a Scrope of commanding figure, who moved – high in station and powerful in person – across the early scene of English history."

In the whole roll of British peerage there is perhaps no one family whose annals give so many romantic incidents, so many startling episodes. Burke says "The House of Scrope, ennobled in two branches, Scrope of Bolton and Scrope of Masham and Upsall, and its members shared the glory of all the great victories of the Middle Ages. The Scropes have an unbroken descent from the Conquest, if not from the time of Edward the Confessor."

Very pleasant too were the days at Carlton-in-Cleveland. All the time I was gaining experience and knowledge which was to stand me in such good stead as a sporting writer. Squire George Sutton, told me much of past sporting tradition and I was frequently at Potto Grange with Fred Horsfall.

I went the round of the Northern race meetings and in the summer of 1908 Fred Horsfall, Walter Pearson and I had a very pleasant week touring Bilsdale, Farndale, Bransdale and the Helmsley district on horseback. Walter Pearson was agent for Lord Mexborough's Hawnby estate and his brother "Nimrod" was for many years secretary of the Sinnington Hunt. We visited hunt kennels, called on sportsmen, saw studs and played a joke on Colonel George Scoby, who had a Cleveland Bay stud at Beadlam near Helmsley. I didn't know him then and Walter Pearson sent a wire that he was bringing a South African millionaire to buy Clevelands. I found that I was to impersonate the millionaire. Col. Scoby had a very good lunch ready for us and decanted some of his best vintage port. He did not find out that he had been hoaxed until the Yorkshire Show at Huddersfield a few weeks later, when someone introduced us. In later years I did buy Clevelands to export to Africa, Canada, America and Japan.

I think the first time I attended Stokesley Show was in 1903. Anyway that year is the first catalogue I possess and from it I see Sir Robert Ropner was president and the Stokesley Volunteer Brass Band played during the afternoon. Stokesley Show had not then eclipsed its parent, the Cleveland Show, but it was becoming more and more popular with farmers and sportsmen and with the townspeople of Teesside — which has stood the show in such good stead financially. In those days Stokesley Show was still essentially for the benefit of agricultural progress and without any of the catch-penny, circus, fun-of-the-fair extraneous attractions to draw those who do not know one breed of horse or cattle from another. The leaping classes were the only "extra" on the programme and they had their origin, not as the most important event, but as a test that hunters were able to do their job. It is very interesting to add – which few people know – that both horse leaping classes and hound shows had their origin in the Cleveland Show when Tom Parrington, then Secretary, introduced them. He started both classes at the Yorkshire Show too, later on when he became secretary. In the ridden hunter classes the competitors had to jump a fence into the ring where the judges were waiting for them. Nowadays jumping is the biggest attraction at agricultural shows and has become a profession. Somehow it has never had much appeal to me. There seems something artificial about popping horses over fences in cold blood in a show ring, with many of those in the saddle adopting most remarkable positions.

I was becoming more and more interested in horse racing and was very friendly with Matt Peacock who used to hunt regularly with the local packs. I often went with him to his father's delightful Manor House at Middleham and renewed my close friendship with Bob Colling. Of the 112 books that I have written none gave me more pleasure than *Malton Memories and I'Anson Triumphs*, my life story of William I'Anson. Bob Colling rode for I'Anson for many years and married the daughter of Robert I'Anson, brother of William. I knew Bob's sons Jack and George when they were youngsters. We young men worshipped Robert I'Anson, of whom the Hon. George Lambton said: "No better man over fences and hurdles ever lived, and I think he was the most popular man of his day with the public." Robert would give us the best advice about riding in the nicest possible way. His grandsons Jack and George quickly made their mark as jockeys. They inherited not only the skill and character of their grandfather but also, unfortunately, his length of leg and height, so their racing days were prematurely cut short.

Both Jack and his younger brother George were apprenticed

to their father when he started training at Spigot Lodge. His first patron was Viginti Thompson, connected with Wearside shipping, who later moved to Hampshire. It was Thompson who, in 1917, persuaded Bob Colling – much against his inclinations – to leave his beloved Yorkshire for Newmarket. Bob started to train at Newmarket and his first winner was Buckthorne at Hurst Park. For years he was associated with the Astor family, though at the outset of his career as a trainer, his principal patron was the wealthy American, Charles Garland, who made his mark as a polo player as well as on the Turf. He owned Somme Kiss. When Mr. Garland died in 1921 he left the Scaltback Stud and property to Bob.

Throughout Jack Colling's jockey days, he was handicapped by increasing weight. He was only eleven years old when, in 1911, he rode his first winner, Manque, owned by F. Stobart. This success was scored at Gosforth Park where his father had notched his initial winner in 1889. Jack had very bad luck to meet a brilliant horse in the odds-on favourite Gainsborough in the First World War substitute Derby at Newmarket. He was second on Lord Astor's 100-8 chance Blink, and Gainsborough went on to complete the Triple Crown.

Jack Colling owned the 5,000-acre Scargill estate on the Yorkshire side of Teesdale, with its good grouse moors. I believe Jack's heart had always been in Yorkshire and know that when he decided to leave Newmarket he would like to have taken the historic Hambleton training quarters. The plan did not materialise and he went to West Ilsley where Dick Hern succeeded him as trainer to Lord Astor and his brother.

Jack always had bias towards Yorkshire courses on which he made annual – and usually profitable – raids. I remember the Hon. J. J. Astor once remarking to me "My horses seem to win most of their races at North Country meetings which I am unable to attend. I like Yorkshire and I have a suspicion that my excellent trainer likes it even better and loves an excuse to get back there to race, to shoot and to hunt."

CHAPTER THREE

HAMBLETON

Frequent visits to the stables run by John Osborne, Dobson Peacock and Bob Colling, made me long all the more to enter fully into this way of life. So, late in 1903 I moved to Bedale and gained experience for several months at a stud farm nearby. The following year I went to Hambleton — and began one of the happiest periods of my long life, learning the mysteries and the joys of the racehorse training art with Jim Adams.

I could not have gone anywhere that had a richer, longer, or more interesting Turf history — or had a tutor more skilled than Jim Adams. I worked as hard as any stableman, "doing" two horses as they should be done. Up at dawn to get the first lot out before the heat of the day in summer, riding schools over the excellent steeplechase course in winter and then often hunting all day with the Bilsdale or Sinnington hounds when there was no race meeting to attend. Jim Adams had forgotten more about horses, training, and Turf politics than most of the present generation of trainers will ever know. He was descended from a family which for generations had been in the horse trade and connected with racing and I learned a lot from him. He had thirty or forty horses at Hambleton when I joined him.

The first thoroughbred I owned was a filly, Batty, bred by Frank Wrightson, a Stokesley man who had a butcher's business in Stockton until he turned bookmaker. I used her for leading work over hurdles at Hambleton and she was a wonderful schoolmaster. I remember we bought a couple of cheap horses at the Thirsk autumn meeting which had shown a bit of form. Riding Batty I led them in training spins and within a month they both won over hurdles.

The first racehorse I rode was Hambleton Queen (by Queen's Birthday, out of Heather Queen), bred by Major R. B. Turton, of Kildale Hall. She was third at Shincliffe and a few weeks later was beaten by a neck at Wetherby, when favourite.

Riding schooling with Bob, Jim and Dave Adams, all good jockeys and fine horsemen — was always a bit hectic. Both Jim and Dave were deaf and Bob not given to suffering fools and beginners gladly. As we went round the steeplechase course one would shout to me "Pull to the right!" another would shout "Pull to the left," Jim would yell "Don't gan so fast," followed immediately by an order from Bob "Send the buggers at their bloody fences." Amid all these contradictory instructions it was impossible to know what to do to be right. And, when we had pulled up, loosened girths and were walking the horses round, Bob not infrequently pointed to me and said "That's t'warst of putting dammed jays up!" I remember the first school I rode, Bob told me before we started "Toss that cosh stick away! It's as much as you can do to ride with your hands!"

There was no likelihood of a beginner getting conceited or fancying himself as a horseman when riding in gallops with the Adams brothers! What artists they were in the saddle and in stables too! Despite all their skill, all their knowledge and their ability not only to get horses fit but to know when they were fit and where to place them, none of the brothers ever gave me the impression of really loving horses. They never knocked any of them about but they believed in being absolute masters — and letting horses know that they were. They were strict, even harsh, in stables and often had horses frightened of them. Sometimes they spoke a kindly word to a horse which had just won, or when particularly pleased with an animal they had dressed over. They were of the old school, and spent a lot of time wisping and "doing" horses. This was counted as one of the most important parts of the science of training and I am sure the Adams brothers were right.

Today trainers cannot get lads to really put their weight behind wisps and body-brushes for at least an hour at morning and evening stables. As Matt Peacock said to me: "They stroke them as though they were playing with their best girls' hair and that's no use for muscling horses up." But with all their careful stable management I never knew the brothers show any real affection for a horse. Pride, yes! – but never any sentiment. There was no kindly word, no lumps of sugar, no kissing of a horse's muzzle. They were firm disciplinarians both with horses and apprentices.

Jim Adams had 30 horses owned by George Drake, the Leeds bookmaker, who raced as "G.W. Smith". He imported an American jockey named Elmer James who "was paid and did as he was told," often without the trainer knowing what the jockey WAS told.

I soon had a horse or two of my own in training and a half-share in others, and was as happy as a sandboy. I rode two or three horses every morning in training gallops over the excellent steeplechase course then laid on the first moor on which our stables, afterwards occupied by Noel Murless and now by Jack Calvert, were built.

During the first summer I was at the historic Hambleton training quarters, trainer Jim Adams' father, then a well-known Northern horse dealer, asked me if I would like to accompany him and another dealer called Harry Brand, to some of the Yorkshire horse fairs. This was just up my street. So, in 1904, I had a memorable, educative and altogether delightful experience of horse fairs, still in their zenith and with little indication that the horse was soon to be out-moded on the land and on the road. One of the first horse fairs we went to was Topcliffe, near Thirsk, to which Adams – "Old Jim" as he was called to differentiate him from his trainer son, who was still called "Young Jim" when he was ninety – sent over 35 horses. He was prepared to buy twice as many more, for both he and Brand had contracts to supply several corporations, some London haulage firms and a number of undertakers.

As an example of the number of horses required in towns at that period, James McKinley — who was responsible for Harry Peacock's start as a trainer in 1931 — never had less than 1,000 horses in his Glasgow stables. He supplied funeral coaches, the police, fire brigade and used many for charabanc work. Harry made a good start as trainer for McKinley, winning him the 1932 Lincolnshire Handicap with Jerome Fendor.

We passed Adams' string of 35 horses on our way to Topcliffe. Their heads were tied to the tails of the horses in front and there were only two men in charge of the lot. One of the men was a most amusing gipsy character, who I never knew by any other name than "Fad". He was up to all the tricks in the trade — and there were a good many at horse fairs!

The whole scene and atmosphere was one of noise, clamour and quite unlike anything I had previously experienced at other horse sales. Horses were galloped and trotted up Topcliffe's one street to show their paces. Little knots of swarthy-skinned gipsies, cracking their whips, haggling and bartering, added to the pandemonium. The present generation can never experience what "all the fun of the fair" meant in those days of 70 years ago at places like Seamer, Topcliffe, Northallerton, Brough Hill, Yarm and other ancient horse fairs. It was during that round of fairs that I became interested in some of the gipsy clans. Like their forbears they went from fair to fair, selling and swapping horses while their womenfolk added to the precarious family income by hawking lace, or clothes-pegs. These were really a cloak for telling fortunes and buying cheap farm produce to add to the rabbits and hares caught by the lurchers attached to every caravan.

These fairs still continue but mainly in "pleasure" fairs though there may be an odd horse or two. In those days there were big droves of unbroken fell ponies brought to Yarm fair from Brough Hill. Then, the main street at places like Yarm and Topcliffe were lined both sides with horses and every stall at the inns were filled. Many of the horses were sound, useful animals, though it was an understood thing that these fairs offered an opportunity to get rid of "mistetched" animals, kickers, jibbers, unsound or with some "if" about them. The gipsy fraternity could alter the teeth markings to make horses appear years younger than they were. They could put life for a day into a decrepit jade and could doctor lame animals so that they trotted sound on fair day. The long-whip, silver-ringed, tight-trousered caravan-folk were known as "The Forty Thieves" and in those days had horse-drawn caravans. Now they travel in expensive motor vans. I got to know some of them quite well, learned a good deal from them and liked them a lot. For over 300 years they have been harried, persecuted and suspected. They certainly poached a bit and have always been restless wanderers, but have not deserved half the charges brought against them.

Attending those horse fairs was an experience I would not have missed. I also went the round of the principal Irish horse fairs. Charles Brotherton wanted me to buy him some Irish horses in 1905. I told him that the Irish dealers knew practically every horse worth anything in the country and if they hadn't got hold of all the best animals long before the fairs, then they would meet them a mile or two away and secure them there.

However, Mr. Brotherton was sure we could pick up some bargains. With him money was not a consideration. I had an open cheque book, and a free-hand. He booked suites of rooms at Mallow and elsewhere. At Cahirmee (Buttevant) Fair, as I expected, we got nothing. It was the same at Clonmel and Tipperary. Eventually we came home without making a purchase and Harry Rose provided the horses he wanted.

The Irish horse fairs are in many respects like Brough Hill, Topcliffe and Yarm used to be. They, too, have their gipsy contingent, and every sale seems to be celebrated by drinking "luck" in pint pots of porter, well seasoned with pepper.

Harry Rose I knew all my life and I cannot think of anyone who has had a longer or more varied connection with the Turf both at home and on the Continent. He never missed a North country meeting and invariably wore a pair of gold and enamel cuff-links depicting his 1896 winner, Straight Shot, over fences at the Malton meeting. Harry, of Otterington House, Northallerton was then a boy of 15 at St. Peter's School, York. He was born at Malton in 1881. His father owned racehorses and Harry was reared in a Turf and "horsey" atmosphere becoming a polished horseman. As an amateur rider at home and on the Continent, in the hunting field and point-to-points, in the show-ring — both as exhibitor and judge — and as a trainer too, he distinguished himself. Harry spent some years with W. Gilbert, a successful trainer at Malvern, then took some horses to the Continent and won a lot of races in Germany, Holland, Belgium and Austria. He rode them as an amateur, frequently returning to this country to buy fresh horses for himself and for foreign sportsmen. I fancy Harry rode the first horse Charles Elsey ever ran over fences. This was Baker's Lad at the, now defunct, Hall Green (Birmingham) meeting in 1910 and it gave Harry one of the worst falls he ever had. A retriever dog ran onto the course, upsetting horse and rider — and what was reckoned "a good thing." On returning permanently to England he started to train a few 'chasers at Harrogate. Later he trained for some years at Spofforth, near Wetherby, one of his best horses, being Tallow Knight, which won him a lot of races. Finally he moved to Otterington and continued to train there until the outbreak of the Second World War. Afterwards he had a horse occasionally with Harry Peacock.

I have never cared much for shooting, and disliked the wholesale slaughter of driven birds. When a pupil with Jim Adams, though, I was once or twice invited to join a syndicate which leased the Hambleton shooting in 1906. The syndicate consisted of Prince Ranjitsinghi, Lord Hawke and Percy Tew, all great cricketers at that time. When the Prince came to shoot, he stayed with the Rev. Borrisow, then vicar of Gilling but previously his tutor at Oxford. A lot of pheasants were reared for them and there were some excellent drives in Flaxendale, quite near the training stables. The Prince was a good shot. He had an Indian servant who loaded for him and prepared his food in accordance with the religious sect to which he belonged.

The Prince was taken with my very well bred steeplechaser, John Dory, by Isinglass out of a Bend Or mare. He thought he would be an imposing mount for him on ceremonial occasions. I was very ready to sell at a tenth the price I mentioned to His Highness. He seemed keen, though, and came to the stables to have a ride on him. I saw he was a bit nervous, but I assured him that John Dory was the quietest horse in the world, that he had a good mouth, and was "a kid's mount" which needed urging on rather than holding back. Unfortunately for some reason John Dory did not approve of having an Indian potentate on his back. Before we got out of the stableyard for the Prince to have a canter on the first moor John Dory gave a couple of playful bucks which landed His Highness on the grass. Nothing could persuade him to mount again, so the sale was off. I could have done with the money, which I thought was as good in my pocket — emptier than usual. John Dory was the best bred horse I ever owned, for Isinglass was the racer of the century and the best of his year at two, three, four and five years old. He won the 1893 Two Thousand Guineas, Derby and St. Leger, and was beaten only once during his career. The Isinglass achievement of 11 victories from 12 starts earned £57,455 in stake money which remained the record until 1952. He is still the only horse to win the Triple Crown, Eclipse Stakes and Ascot Gold Cup. His only defeat was by Raeburn in the Lancashire Plate.

Life was always exciting at Hambleton — and the stable coups were often substantial. I can still remember vividly one such coup, and every detail of the extraordinary happenings on that beautiful Spring morning in 1909.

The training stable at Hambleton was awake and astir much earlier than usual. We wanted to be out before the world was awake so that we could try a well-bred colt called Toronto, by Fitzsimon, without the touts or anyone outside the stable knowing anything about the gallop. The moor is an isolated place and eight miles from a town and railway station. Here, if anywhere, we thought that stable secrets could be preserved. It proved otherwise, however, although I do not know to this day how the carefully arranged plans leaked out.

A well-known owner lent us a horse with good recent form with which to try Toronto, and came out himself to see the gallop.

The loaned horse arrived at Thirsk station in the dark and reached Hambleton mountain top in darkness and unobserved so far as we knew. Only Jim Adams and the owner knew its identity. We stole out of the stable yard that early April morning without a sound. Usually apprentice jockeys and stableboys are whistling, or talking to the animals they are riding on the way to the gallops. Ours was rather like a funeral procession. There were two reasons for this. First and foremost we wanted no one to know what was in the wind; secondly we had decided to use part of a straight five furlongs gallop rented by another Hambleton trainer. Now it should be explained that to get five furlongs, this other trainer was compelled to use part of our gallop. We naturally thought we had the right to use his stretch of turf. To have asked his permission, however, would have meant destroying the very secrecy we wished to preserve. So we had decided to take French leave on the expectation that one good turn deserves another.

I was a nice light-weight in those days and rode a mare called Buoyantly in the stripped gallop. We all left the gate together and Toronto, as we hoped would be the case, won the trial easily. As no one except his owner and trainer knew the weights we all carried, the gallop did not convey very much to any but those two, beyond the fact that the leggy and by no means good-looking Toronto, had won. We could see, however, by the faces of those who did know, that they were more than satisfied with the result. No sooner had we dismounted, loosened the girths on the horses we had ridden, and begun to circle them round for a few minutes to let them get their wind and settle down, than two burly figures appeared from behind a wall. Somehow they must have known about the trial and that we were to use the other trainer's portion of the gallop. They approached with all the haste and importance of Scotland Yard men about to make a big capture. Producing a notebook, one of the men first tackled Dave Adams who was very deaf. "I want your name and address" said the man with a book. But Dave didn't hear him and went on walking his horse round. The demand was repeated with no better result. Eventually the question was shouted and Dave replied: "Who are you? What do you want my name for?"

"I'm a detective" was the answer.

"Then if you are a detective it's your business to find out," retorted Dave, who declined further converse. Then the detective approached the trainer, and demanded his name and address.

"Why do you want it?" asked Jim.

"Because you have been trespassing on someone else's ground" was the reply.

"Then if that's so" was the quiet retort, "You are trespassing now on my private gallop, which has regularly been used by the man whom I suppose has employed you. You've no right here — get out!"

The detectives evidently saw that we were not to be terrorised like country bumpkins so departed to summon the aid of the local police from Helmsley, some eight miles away. We had a visit from them later in the day, and you would have thought that murder had been committed at Hambleton. This storm in a teacup was caused by the other jealous Hambleton trainer who meanly objected to the Adams brothers using his stretch of the five furlongs gallop.

As for me I did not see the police because there was another thrill in store for me that morning. When our detective visitors left I was preparing to mount a big steeplechase horse called Jackdaw Crag to ride a school over fences. A boy held his own horse, Buoyantly, with one hand and tried to give me a leg-up onto Jackdaw Crag with his other hand. Before I was into the saddle Jackdaw Crag reared, then buck jumped, and the big-peaked cap I was wearing came right over my eyes blinding me. I felt with my feet for the stirrup irons and got one in but by this time Jackdaw Crag had bolted. I could not see and the next thing I knew was that he was in the air. I thought he had made another buck till he pecked and I found myself on the ground at the edge of a dry ditch — "the open grave," as steeplechase jockeys call it!

Away went Jackdaw Crag with me hung up in the one stirrup. He kicked at me as he galloped and landed one or two well-aimed shots in my ribs. It is said of one knight of yore who had a bad fall of this sort, "Between the stirrup and the ground, he mercy sought and mercy found."

Well, I never was so afraid in my life. Bruised and battered, I was clattered along the ground — fortunately it was the thick turf for which Hambleton has long been famous — kicked at and entirely helpless. Certainly I put in a few quick "Hail Mary's" that the stirrup leather would break. I knew that was my only chance, as those who see a man being dragged are absolutely helpless. If they gallop after a horse which is dragging someone they only make him increase his pace. If they try to turn him the odds are they will send the unfortunate victim under the legs of the excited animal, which probably does not understand what it is he is trailing by his side. I know of no situation more terrifying, and none in which spectators are more anxious to do something, yet quite unable. I quite expected that my number was up and that I should soon land a mangled mass. I would not like to live those dreadful seconds again. I was a youth then, and thought little of falls. Indeed, sometimes I rode for a fall, courting and expecting it. To be dragged, however, is another matter. The bravest man in the world trembles at the thought of that and prays he may be freed from such an experience. Had I been on a hard road I should probably have been soon unconscious but as it was I saw those long legs of Jackdaw Crag's going faster and faster. I saw his polished shoes as they were lifted and as they struck at me in an attempt to get rid of the burden the horse had attached to him. He wasn't nearly as anxious to be free from me as I was to be free from him. At last the stirrup leather was torn from the saddle and I lay on the ground with the sky spinning like a roundabout at a fair. I was quite sure that I hadn't a whole bone left in my body, that I should be weeks and weeks in hospital and, worse than all, that I should possibly never ride again. Those were my first thoughts after I had breathed gratitude to my guardian angel. Up came some of those who had stood breathlessly watching.

Captain Whaley-Thompson – who owned Jackdaw Crag and was to ride him a few days later at the, now defunct, Shincliffe meeting in the County of Durham – was the first to reach me. "Are you much the worse?" he asked.

"Where's the horse?" I replied.

"Vanished into the blue," said he. "Never mind about him. Let's get you back to the house. I wouldn't have given tuppence for your life, when I saw him making for that stone wall."

No sooner had the stirrup-leather come away from the saddle than Jackdaw Crag had jumped the stone wall into a wood, galloped through it, jumped the stone wall on the other side out on to the high road, and then gone best pace down Kilburn Bank – a very steep place, as motorists know – nearly to Coxwold. A roadman caught him and tied him to a gate, where he was quietly eating grass when one of the stable lads – who had followed his footprints – came on the scene to reclaim him. Despite his mad gallop through the thickly-planted wood and down the road there was not a scratch on the horse, and he was none the worse. As for myself, a doctor from Oswaldkirk was sent for and found I had a dislocated ankle, a cracked rib or two, and a good many black, blue and purple bruises.

This did not end the series of thrills. The summonses for trespass arrived in due course, and so did the Stockton Spring Meeting, to which I hobbled, a very stiff and broken down youth. Toronto was in the Carlton Selling Handicap, which was thought to be a good thing for him. He had been bought at York sales for a mere song by Elmer James. Toronto ran in my racing colours — and George McCall was engaged to ride him. It was decided that the trial and our expectations should be kept a deep, dead secret. We wouldn't even tell our best pals, and we wouldn't have a penny on the course. All the stable money would be distributed in tenners to S.P. offices all over the country. But was it a secret? The very dogs barked Toronto at the street corners, and when we arrived in the paddock someone, who asked me about the horse replied to my evasive answers: "You needn't be so dammed close and mysterious, look at this!" He pulled a tipster's printed sheet from his pocket and showed me in big capitals "Toronto XXX. Best thing of the week."

In view of all the secrecy — rigidly observed by me as a matter of honour — this was really a mystery, and remained so. I never knew how it got out. There were nine entries and nine runners. Toronto started favourite at 6 to 4 — though he had never previously won a race, and, so far as that goes, never won another. McCall often told me that the race was one of the biggest thrills he had during his long and brilliant career. Although the official return gives Toronto as only winning by 10 lengths, I don't think I ever saw a horse win by much further on the flat than he did at Stockton that day. George — who always had a man's strength and head with a boy's weight — had to put two pounds extra and rode 7st 12lbs instead of 7st 10lbs. They were a bad lot of horses — they must have been — for Toronto made hacks of them. It wasn't a race; it was a procession, and those who have backed a horse well know what a thrill it gives them to see the animal they have supported come romping home. It was a wonderful and memorable day — the culminating thrill of a series of thrills. As I have said,

Toronto never won another race afterwards. This was a day one lives again and again in memory, not so much because of gain as the satisfaction which comes with conquest, and especially when one has played a part in the preparation. Then it tickles a very human and forgiveable vanity and enables one to say "I told you so!"

Not all my memories of Stockton's racecourse are happy, though. A few years later I walked away from the meeting, swearing that I would never race there again. I did so because of an insult to Bob Robson. He had paid thousands of pounds in entry fees at Stockton during his long career as a trainer. The year after Bob retired he and Bob Colling were staying with me for the Teesside fixture. I rang up T. H. Hitch, clerk of the course, to declare some colours for Colling and asked him to put Robson's name down at the owner's gate. This he did for the first day but crossed it off for the second day, so that Bob was refused admission. He was both hurt and embarrassed but went and paid. I was furious and was telling Hitch that the past counted for something and that it was an insult both to Robson and myself, when Dr. Hind, one of Stockton Race Committee, came up and heard what had happened. He said "Come with me." We followed him to the owner's and trainer's gate, and the doctor told Sykes, the gateman "Whenever Mr. Robson comes to this meeting he is to be admitted as one of the most honoured and welcome guests." This annoyed Hitch, who sarcastically thanked me for helping him to manage his meeting. Half-an-hour later a small trainer asked me if I could get Charlie Ringstead to ride for him. I went into the weighing-room to ask Ringstead if he was free to ride in the race. When I was talking to him Hitch came in, interrupted the conversation, and told me I had no right there. I retorted that I would leave the weighing-room at once and also the course, and would never again set foot on it. I have never since been to a race-meeting on the Teesside course.

In 1906 Picton, owned by Lionel Dugdale of Crathorne Hall and named after the nearby village, was very strongly fancied for the Derby. I lunched with Mr. Dugdale at Crathorne Hall a day or two before the race and was then told the colt had developed a leg. His owner was present when Leach, the Newmarket "vet", examined him. Afterwards Mr. Dugdale asked the "vet" what his fee was, wrote him out a cheque and asked: "What do you advise?" The reply was, "Pray for rain." I don't know whether the prayers were offered but the rain didn't come.

Mr. Dugdale had just moved to the new Crathorne Hall. Indeed, the wiring for electricity had just been finished and it was planned that the whole place was to be a blaze of light and illuminations when the news came through that Picton had won the Derby. It was not to be! Picton, ridden by Mr. (afterwards Sir) George Thursby an amateur rider, was beaten into second place by Danny Maher on Spearmint. If rain had come, or if Picton had been a sound horse, it is hardly likely he would have beaten Spearmint. Sir George commenting years later on the winner wrote to me: "I consider Spearmint one of the best modern horses, comparable with any of the smashers of the past. In the 1906 Derby he beat me without effort, though Picton was a really good colt. Danny Maher told me towards the end of his life that Spearmint was the best horse he ever rode."

On his way home from Epsom Mr. Dugdale's train was held up at Harrogate and the squire of Crathorne told the station master that if the delay was much longer he would miss his connection for Picton. The rail official — obviously speaking through his pocket — retorted: "There are lots of folks in Yorkshire who wish Picton had missed the connection for Epsom!"

Sir George had three Derby rides, coming second not only in 1906 on Picton, but also in 1904. Riding for his half-brother, Sir John Thursby, on John O'Gaunt he was unlucky to be beaten by St. Amamt, ridden by K. Cannon.

I remember in this connection a bet made by one well-known Turfite who refused to believe that any amateur rider within living memory had ridden three times in the Derby and had twice been second. He, of course, lost his wager. He was not ready either to believe that several other amateurs have had mounts in the Derby, again showing that either his education in Turf history had been neglected, or that he had not a very retentive memory. In 1837 Mr. Bartley, an Oxford-street bootmaker, rode his own horse, Pegasus, in the Derby. Mr. W. Robinson, a Richmond (Yorks) solicitor, owner and breeder, in 1858 took the mount on his own Pellister, and in 1869 Mr. W. Bevill rode Lord Royston's Alpenstock into fourth place in the Derby. He had also ridden in the 1862 Derby. In later years he managed Lord St. Vincent's horses at Telscombe, and later became clerk of the course at Kempton Park.

Throughout the years that I was at Hambleton George Drake was the stable's chief patron, but later he built Warwick Lodge stables at Middleham and had his horses there. He was not an easy man to train for. He was suspicious, looked on horses as machines, and insisted on having his own way. He was financially interested in theatres, boxers and greyhounds and became one of the stalwarts on the rails, ready to lay £1,000 or more without blinking an eyelid.

There was a most amusing character named John Dent. He had a useful chestnut mare called Lucy II, which his brother trained at Fighting Cocks, near Darlington. I fancy they had a farm there and that Dent had a butcher's business at Middlesbrough. They were tall, burly men and the trainer's brother used to lead Lucy round the parade ring when she ran, while John — in an outsize black Homburg hat — did the talking and worked the commission in the ring. Lucy II won at Stockton in 1909, and the same season was successful at Newcastle and Haydock Park. I remember a Newmarket trainer asking me at Newcastle if I could buy Lucy for him. I approached Dent, whose reply was "Efter what she's deean tidaay, all t'money i' Ingerland wadn't buy her."

It is said that we are all equal on the Turf and under it and

John was one of those genial, amusing fellows, looking like anything but one of the racing or "horsey" men, who go to make up the strange Turf army. Some of them are better sportsmen at heart than those who spend hundreds of thousands on bloodstock and own classic winners. John Dent was a genuine sportsman. He bred Lucy II out of a mare of doubtful pedigree, called Panzerona, which as a two-year-old won him a couple of races with old Seth Chandley in the saddle. The first of these was at Edinburgh. Three days earlier she was second favourite at Lanark with little Tommy Lofthouse riding. She was last in a field of five but at Edinburgh, when again second favourite, she won by half a length. The local stewards were a bit suspicious, could not accept Dent's explanation and he had to appear before the Jockey Club Stewards, who believed every word he said, and sent him back home triumphant. John died in 1923.

The late Etienne de Mestre, an Australian friend of the Woottons, was appointed in charge of Drake's horses at Middleham. At that time George Formby was apprenticed to Drake's stable. Formby's father was a real racing enthusiast and most anxious for George to become a jockey. Apart from increasing weight, though, George lacked the God given gift of hands and horsemanship. He tried hard but finally followed his father on the Music Hall round. George's subsequent career is a legend. He would have been very lucky to have hit such high spots on the Turf.

I well remember the split between de Mestre and Drake. At York races in 1911 the trainer backed one of the stable's horses without telling the owner. The horse won but Drake did not have a penny on. There was an explosion — both were hot tempered men — and they parted company at a moment's notice.

"Eddie" de Mestre bought the grey Hospodar and another horse at the York meeting so that he could start training on his own. I was staying with Bob Robson, and he offered de Mestre and his horses "hospitality" until he found stables. They soon came to loggerheads, however, because the Australian was not a real horse lover like Bob. He sometimes lost his temper with horses and was severe. This did not suit Robson, a great horseman and a most lovable and tender-hearted man, who always followed his father's advice: "Get the best horses you can into the worst company you can. But keep the best company yourself."

I was sufficiently in de Mestre's confidence — and not many were — for him to often show me some foreign bark which, when diluted with an egg-cupful of water, had a remarkably stimulating effect on horses. The mixture was given to runners an hour before a race and really did work wonders with sluggish horses. It was said to beat all "dope" tests and to have no after effects. Certainly it worked well for de Mestre. Actually the Americans introduced chemical dopes into England. Before that it was quite common to see English trainers openly give a "pep" mixture to their horses in the paddocks. This was often simply a good shot of whisky, or half-a-bottle of port. The Hon. George Lambton brought the whole doping business to a head in 1903. He told his brother, Lord Durham, then a Jockey Club member, that he was going to expose the growing practice by "doping" a horse called Folkestone. He took this course to force the Jockey Club to take action. George Lambton said of Folkestone: "He was always last in a race, and was one of the biggest rogues in training. I first 'doped' him in a trial and he astounded me. He jumped off in front and won in a canter." Again "doped" Folkestone was sent to Pontefract where he easily beat a field of twelve and nearly went round again before jockey Joe Plant could pull him up. It was a selling race and Bob Robson bought Folkestone for 120 guineas. He was later rather sore that Lambton — with whom he had often ridden as an amateur — had not told him that the horse had been "doctored". Afterwards Folkestone was sent hurdling and won a small race or two.

Joe Plant — the Pocket Hercules — gave up riding after the First World War. Later he had a part in a racing film. I saw him at Warwick races some years later. He then had no idea that the winner he rode at Pontefract had been doped.

Harry Taylor, who later rode Folkestone hurdling, knew all about a horse called Sporran having been given the "needle" before a Cartmel 'chase. That horse was lame on arrival and Taylor wired his owner that it would be impossible for him to run. Instructions came back that Jimmy Deans, the well-known North country racing vet, was on his way to treat Sporran. "I weighed out" recalled Taylor. "I was about to mount Sporran when Mr. Deans came along, gave the horse an injection in the shoulder with a syringe. Sporran was a quiet old horse, but he was at once on his toes and all signs of lameness were gone. By the time the flag dropped he was mad and uncontrollable. He won as he liked and I believe was the first doped horse to score over fences." In those days, when "doping" was not illegal, Jimmy Deans had a number of trainer patrons who regularly bought "speedy balls" and other medicine. He died in 1930 shortly after making a public statement: "I was the first veterinary surgeon to attempt the hypodermic injection of a stimulant into a racehorse before running. I confidently assert that it is possible to treat a horse by this method, not once but many times, without detrimental effect either immediately or in the future."

A Stockton owner, Andrew Robinson, had quite a lot of horses in training with his nephew Ossy Casebourne. His brother Vernon rode for a few seasons as a professional jockey and they began training at Yarm, then bought a farm at Picton and trained there until taking quarters at Middleham. On their Picton farm they laid down a racecourse and had a meeting for a few years under National Hunt Rules. The capital was found by them, Andrew Robinson, Barz Riley, C. J. Martin and Dick Gaunt and one or two others. Picton Races were never a success and, beyond the one stand, had no amenities of any kind. Michael Pigg — who had for several years been right hand man for Miles I'Anson, and followed him as clerk of course at Ripon — was the first Picton clerk of the course. Later the position was offered to me but I declined. I attended all the meetings at Picton and fancy they hold a record in that at the 1914 fixture, only 13 runners turned up for the six races. There was no more racing after 1915.

An outstanding Turfite at this period, was Tom Devereux who had owned a lot of horses and had his finger in many varied pies. He was a man with a wealth of experience and most interesting memories. Devereux — who died in 1928 at the age of 81 — was a bit of an autocrat, tall, distinguished-looking, quick-tempered, and not too easy to get on with. He had in turn been owner, commissioner for big stables and leading jockeys, promoter for prize fights, financier for professional cyclists and running men, speculator in property, tobacconist, antique dealer and inn-keeper. For some years he had the White Hart Inn and founded the Victoria Club adjoining in Dovecot-street, Stockton, where he also owned the Alhambra Music Hall. He started making a book at the age of 20 and was the first bookmaker in the North to have telegrams sent him from the course giving runners and then results. In the early eighties he was racing horses at meetings all over the North, and winning his share of races too.

In 1883 he had a successful time with his Stockton runners and gave the local jockey, Willie Warne his first ride in public on Verona. Warne became one of the leading jockeys in England and in 1895 went to Germany where he rode 750 winners up to the time of the outbreak of the First World War. He was interned and then returned to England at the end of hostilities and died at Newmarket in 1952.

Later, of course, Stockton was to be the scene of Joe Thwaites first race ride. In his day Joe was such a successful jockey. I remember him telling me an amusing story when I went to see him in hospital after a bad accident he had when riding at Stockton. He was for a time in a critical condition and a stableman from Malton who went to "cheer him up" did so by saying "Well, Joe, if the worst comes to the worst and you pop off, you have the satisfaction of knowing you'll have the biggest bloody funeral there's ever been in Malton." Joe lived several years after that. Latterly, though, he was a saddened man and never set foot on a racecourse after his trainer's licence was withdrawn. I always thought he was keener on both football and billiards than racing and remember him declining rides in the last two races one Saturday at Stockton so that he could slip away to Ayresome Park to see the end of a Middlesbrough match. Joe died at Redcar.

Later still Stockton produced another jockey Richard "Snowy" Fawdon. I remember bringing him home from one Saturday Pontefract meeting when he was a very little apprentice in 1926. When he had served his time with Harvey Leader he went out to South Africa, where he had an uncle who was one of the leading trainers, but the experiment did not prove a success. His grandfather was in stables at Middleham a century ago, so he was born into the racing game. At almost the last Redcar meeting the late Lord Zetland attended, Dick Fawdon brought to show me a gold tie-pin which the Lord Zetland of that day had given his grandfather in 1858 after Vedette (by Voltigeur) had won the Ebor Handicap at York. Fawdon had not only cared for the horse at Middleham, but took him to York. Later, of course, Vedette was sire of the mighty Galopin, winner of the 1875 Derby and sire of St. Simon. I told Lord Zetland about the pin and he asked me to take Fawdon to his private box to speak to him and show him the trophy of long ago.

In January 1911 my old friend Jim Adams was warned off, and this unhappy act was the first link in a chain of events that led to my losing my Judge's licence many years later. The Adams decision still makes me smart — and is to the lasting shame of the Jockey Club. *The Calendar* noted that Jim had been warned off for his riding of the mare Yvette at Nottingham. I took a good deal of trouble to find out the ins and outs of the Jockey Club's London trial of the case at which the only Nottingham official present was Stanley Ford, the judge. The prosecution consisted of about five letters from as many of the local stewards, each of whom made an excuse not to appear. Indeed, it is a fact to say that Adams was convicted by letter. What chance can any one accused have of proving his innocence if he cannot cross-question his accusers? I should like to hear what the Lord Chief Justice would say about such a trial.

The prosecuting letters were each pretty much the same — alleging that the mare did not try. Indeed, both sides seemed to agree to this, and it resolved itself into a question of whether it was the jockey or the mare to blame. Yvette started 13-8 favourite, and a newspaper reported that she was for much of the hurdle race a long way last and seemingly "never out of a canter" but she made up a tremendous lot of ground in the closing stages to finish third. Previous trainers had this to say about her. J. E. Brewer: "I found her a thorough jade both at home and in a race, and at times she refused to go out of a canter." Johnny McGuigan: "the biggest jade that ever looked through a bridle." Peter Hardcastle: "Some days for no apparent reason she would not even canter." Added to this, Taylor M.R.C.V.S. and Heather M.R.C.V.S. each gave Adams a Certificate that the mare was "amiss" on the 12th December 1910 immediately after the race. One of the local Stewards alleged that he watched the race especially as his suspicions were aroused before the event. But Adams had no chance of asking him what suspicions were aroused. Who aroused them? What proof or justification had he for doing so? I repeat that every Nottingham Steward failed to put in an appearance at the inquiry. I think that it is manifestly unfair that a number of Stewards of a meeting should make the worst accusations possible against a jockey, and not one of them turn up in a person to substantiate them.

The Adams affair had other repercussions indicating the National Hunt Committee mentality at that period. I had applied for an amateur rider's licence to ride my own horses and could not understand why this was not at once granted. Then I got a letter from a friend on the National Hunt

Committee, R. F. Meysey-Thompson: "I am sorry to say there is some difficulty about obtaining a licence for you from the National Hunt Committee. On account partly of your connection with the Adams stable. Can you kindly tell me where your horses will be trained in future, for I presume they will no longer remain with the Adams'. If they do so I fear your licence will be refused altogether. They intend to be very particular in future as to whom they grant a licence." After this I indicated that I wanted to train my own horses and was told that I would jeopardise my chances of being granted licences if I continued to press the Adams case as a journalist. So by honestly endeavouring to right a wrong and place an injured man, robbed of his profession, in his true colours, I was at risk. Apparently the National Hunt Stewards decided that, because I dared to criticise them in newspaper articles, I was not a fit and proper person to hold a licence to ride or train my own horses. This seemed too far fetched to be true, but on applying for a licence I received the reply: "Your application for a licence under National Hunt Rules has been before the Committee, but has not been granted."

I noted in my syndicated newspaper column at the time: "I stand today as a sporting journalist who has for years endeavoured to further the interests of racing, as an owner who has lived in racing stables, as a man of education, and yet bearing the stigma of being unfitted to hold a trainer's licence — a man upon whose sporting character there is some black spot. I know of none, and feel sure I could have permission of a number of the foremost racing men, owners, trainers, and masters of hounds, to give their names as referees as to whether or no my conduct in the world of racing and hunting warranted such a stigma. I repeat the question: Are the N.H. Stewards tyrannical? If they are not tyrannical, then they know something regarding my character of which I am ignorant, and which they are at liberty to make public. If none of these considerations have influenced them, their only other explanation is that they cannot bear their action, with regard to the case mentioned, to be criticised. Sport under the N.H. Rules is not in such a flourishing condition that the Stewards can afford to damn the character and position of those who patronise it, and thus make it possible that new patrons will think twice before they enter into a sport governed by men who allow pique, or personal feelings, or mere suspicions, to rule their actions. I was getting together a nice little stable at Middleham. I had three horses coming to me this week, and I should have patronised the Northern meetings more than ever. Now I shall have to engage a trainer, and he will have to apply to the N.H. Stewards to train my horses. Will they give him permission to do so, or will they place me in the position of a man warned off the turf? I love racing, and I have written much in the support of it. I should have been much better off financially if I had never been on a racecourse or owned a racehorse; but I am not, according to the N.H. Stewards, a fit and proper person to hold the permission to train my own horses and those of my friends."

Subsequently I was granted a trainer's licence for my own horses and had great fun with the pony sized Kealsham, Prince V and others. I was happily getting a bigger string together when the First World War blasted so many hopes.

The Jim Adams case had a happy ending too. Jim got his trainer's licence back in 1913, after two years of harrowing worry.

CHAPTER FOUR

WAR

I was breaking in some young horses when the First World War broke out. The people in the Dales seemed almost indifferent to it and thought that we should have the Germans beaten in a few weeks without feeling any pinch locally. I feared that it was going to be a long and ghastly business and how right I was. Wanting to be with horses, and in one of the Yorkshire Regiments, I volunteered for either the Yorkshire Hussars or Yorkshire Dragoons. I was not successful with either choice but was commissioned in the 15/19th (The King's) Hussars and reported to Longmoor Barracks, Hampshire on November 2, 1914.

As a sporting Bohemian I did not take very well to soldiering. I was sent to riding school with Lord Torrington, Percy Woodland, Jack Drake, Dick Morgan and other Turf personalities. Major Lionel Kennard – a good horseman and a most charming man was Squadron Commander. From the start he was most kind to me. Arthur Streaker was my troop leader. He was a big fine fellow but a snobbish devil who did nothing to help me or make things easier for me. Johnny Fullerton, whose father used to have the York and Ainsty Hounds, was one of my best pals to begin with. Jim Joel was at riding school with me, while Jim Montagu, the ex Badsworth M.F.H. had just finished. It was bitterly cold but we lived well. Just before the war my parents had moved into Grove House at Norton. I tried to carry on a bit of writing at first to help my parents at home, but soon had to give this up. I was too retiring and shy at first to be popular.

Among my brother subalterns were some Masters of Hounds and men with considerable reputation in the equestrian world. We, like the jockey troopers, went through riding school and again we had cold water thrown on any vanity we might have had as to ability in the saddle. One amateur rider who had ridden a lot of winners was asked, "Have you ever been on a horse before?" We all found difficulty in coping with the big cavalry saddles and riding without our feet in stirrups. Before we were passed out of riding school, one of our tests was negotiating a lane of miniature fences with folded arms and crossed stirrups.

This was quite a new experience which called for a knee and thigh grip. There were those of us who, when we ended up on the ground, were to frequently hear the cynical remark of Major Percy, the 15th/19th Hussar riding master, "Who told you to dismount?"

Later we were posted to Fermoy in Ireland before going to France in March 1916. We all met at Southampton and embarked. We spent a few days at Rouen before setting off for Belle Eglise. At this stage of the war, when barbed-wire, trenches and shell-holes made cavalry useless, several hussar officers were drafted to artillery brigades to assist with horse management, with the official title of Horsemaster. It had been found that the majority of the younger artillery officers had had no experience of horses and that equine mortality was increasing.

Jim Barry and I were selected to be Horsemasters. Our posting came through. We were attached to the 223rd Brigade, R.F.A. who were part of the Royal Naval Division. Eventually a mule cart came for us after hours of weary waiting. We were taken to Varennes. It was knee deep in filth and we had to sleep in a room with three other officers. Although we were known as Horsemasters, in reality we were stud-grooms. I had the care of nearly 1,000 horses. Poor beggars! They were often standing hock-deep in slush and mud, with soaked rugs on their backs, never able to lie down.

I think we were able to do a worthwhile job. I know I got a good deal of satisfaction out of what I did apart from the fun I had in riding some of the Australian buck jumpers, of which we had a good many at the latter end of the war. Later I was posted North and an hour after my arrival I rode up to the front line. This was my first introduction to the sounds of warfare and to dead lying about unburied. It was very cold and the ground was covered in snow and filth. I was in a tent in an orchard. The horses were mangy and stood belly deep in water and filth. We Horsemasters were not altogether welcome and had to tread very carefully at first. I never saw horses in such a state. Pack, pack, packing ammunition day and night and waiting for hours at dumps for ammunition played havoc with them. My first direct job was to be in charge of 60 remounts, some of them mules with which I had never had any dealings before. I made horse lines in a sunken road by the side of a wood and lost three of the mules the first night. I expected Courts of Inquiry and a rumpus, but it seemed quite a usual occurrence — some other unit had stolen them. To start with I hated and abominated the mules but soon I came to have a very profound respect for them as they carried on under weather and forage conditions which caused horses to die like flies. I used to say that you could follow us when we 'trekked' by our line of dead horses by the road side. Personally I was inclined to think that our veterinary sergeants were a little too handy with their pistols. Of course, it saved them a lot of trouble if a horse was dead beat to shoot it. They could always get sanction from an officer if that was necessary because most of the officers had never had anything to do with horses before the war. Goodness knows what effect this had on Britain's horse breeding superiority in the long term though. Surely it must have been little short of disastrous. I continually tried to get watering conditions improved and extra forage but soon found that the staff were helpless, though anxious to be helpful.

I wanted to get my horses strapped for a couple of hours at

the end of each day and exercised as they had been used to, but you have got to have men born and trained among horses to do this. If I asked for men Sergeant Majors invariably detailed the most useless and notorious shirkers they could discover so that their own work would not suffer. Going to water each day the horses were belly deep in mud and often had to wait an hour or more for their turn.

Finally we left this base and had a trek in the snow with many hardships to a place near Vimy Ridge. We were camped in a wheat field which was soon a bog. We spent Easter Monday there in snow and indescribable filth. Some of the 15/19th Hussars came up near us and I went to see them. They had their horses in a wood and were under little better conditions than our own. Their horses had mange. Conditions for the horses were dreadful. My Diary entry for March 15, 1917 was typical: "27 horses evacuated, 1 died, 3 destroyed." The following week: "42 horses were evacuated, 3 died, and 4 were destroyed." This sad story continued until April 11 when we moved in a blizzard to a site near the front. There we had not a particle of shelter or cover and the next day: "160 horses were evacuated, 6 died and 14 were destroyed because of exposure and exhaustion."

We had very short rations here owing to the difficulties of travel and even on the roads sank to the thighs in mud. If a horse went down with exhaustion it was drowned, and carts and gun carriages would pass over it. After the successful Vimy Ridge attack we were supposed to have a rest. We pulled out, a tired, mudstained rabble and after a cold march of a day or two, we arrived in a bitter snowstorm at Madagascar corner near Arras. There was not a stitch of canvas there for us and the site was just a mud heap, but eventually some tents arrived and we put them up in a blinding snowstorm. My neck was swollen up with the cold and the poor horses were standing shivering. The weather began to look up towards the end of March and beginning of April 1917. After six weeks, during which time I replaced as many horses as possible, we went to Roclincourt which was the nicest camp that we were in all the time I was in France. Roclincourt was nearer the firing line and occasionally we got a shell. I saw Arras shelled regularly every morning. The weather was lovely. We had water troughs in the camp, good horse lines and any amount of excellent lucerne and beet growing on old trenches. This I had gathered and boiled up for the poor conditioned horses. It was very hot in May, there was very little firing and consequently there was little ammunition to take up to the line. I had old barbed wire entanglements cleared so that the horses could graze, though the M.P.'s continually warned me off because they said that I was in full view of the Germans and would draw fire. I really did see horses improve here and thoroughly enjoyed life. We had a little steeplechase course put up, and jumping competitions. We even began to build wooden stabling for the winter, and the men asked if they were booked for life in France. Bricks were obtained from ruined houses for standings. I often went up to headquarters. They had a snug place in a trench not far from Chanticleer Corner and it even had flowers outside the doorway. We went about without tunics and hardly knew that there was a war on. The summer really was lovely and I went on daily with grazing parties to improve the horses. In August 1917 I got away for my first leave home — 10 days. I got into civilian clothes as soon as I could and at Norton was asked by an elderly woman: "Why are you not serving your country?"

Soon I was back in France and found the old disused lines of trenches a mass of red poppies and scarlet pimpernell. I used to wander among the trenches on those lovely summer evenings and there started to write a weekly bulletin for the *Gazette* and the *Hull Times*. These articles brought me shoals of letters from home. My object was to give some comfort to the mothers of serving men and to show that we had some fun in France and that all was not quite as sordid as they imagined.

Before long we entrained for Belgium. After a day or two we moved up by way of Hospital Farm and Dirty Bucket Corner to Seige Corner Camp — a dirty muddy place. Just off the Ypres main road I got headquarters on a respectable bit of ground near a stream and a big old farmhouse. Our forward headquarters were a most unhealthy place, continually shelled and reached across the mud by duck-boards — also continually shelled. If you stepped off the duck-boards to avoid the shells you were drowned in the quagmire. We were bombed regularly every night and one night alone had some men and over twenty horses killed. I begged, stole and sweet-hearted sufficient timber to build stables for all our headquarters horses. Then I got a sick-line stable built and put props down as flooring because we had a lot of horses suffering from disease. The men and horses all lived in the utmost squalor and discomfort. Belgium was in every way terrible and a thousand times worse than France.

On January 1 1918 we moved to the Somme again. It was so cold that the ink froze in the bottle on my makeshift desk and the bombing raids made life all the more unpleasant. In early March I was telephoned at 5 a.m. to send the M.O. up to H.Q. because all the staff had been gassed. I rode over and saw the C.O. who told me that 1,600 people had been gassed the night before. His lips were swollen and he spoke with difficulty. I rode on and saw the staff captain and offered myself for any job — but soon the Germans began their offensive with one of the fiercest bombardments imaginable. In my Diary I wrote: "The shelling — the worst I ever heard — began at 4.45 this morning and is still continuing as I write at 7 p.m. It has been a fierce day. I have no definite news yet about what has happened. I am very weary."

The March retreat started with all its terror and dreadfulness. There was a direct hit on a stable and two officer's horses were killed. A sentry came to report that the Boche had broken through our lines, and was steadily advancing on us, and even then machine-gun bullets were flying round us like hailstones. From that moment thousands of us spent seven or eight days in a veritable hell. I soon had my horses saddled and gave orders to my own men and then galloped on to the 317 Brigade, to see if they had been warned. I walked the roads all night catching stragglers. My groom accompanied me and when we returned to our own lines again — across country and in the dark — we were both nearly shot by our retiring infantry, who mistook us for German cavalry.

During the German breakthrough on the first day, the enemy entered our lines. I was the only officer on the spot so I moved the horses on my own initiative because the Germans had advanced so close. I got out, only a few minutes before the Boche arrived. The roads were pandemonium and the Germans still advancing. So we went back from one place to another. I was left with no officer to help me and wrote in my Diary on March 27: "After four days and nights without sleep I tried to rest in the mess cart. A sentry with nerves kept awakening me to tell me that we were being surrounded by Indians and Germans and being gassed. Crowds of refugees passed me."

We never had our clothes off for a week, rarely slept or ate and went through a period of nerve strain which brought us to such a pitch that we didn't care much if we were killed.

We were shelled daily. The bombardment began at 7.20 and so again did the retreat. The horror of those days was the exhaustion and strain — not of fear of danger, not of what seemed certain death in the long run, but the fear of the unknown and of uncertainty. Time after time we stood to fight or rest and time after time we were compelled by overwhelming numbers to go back, back, back. How we hated retreating! How we wondered if this was an inglorious and crushing end of it all! How our blood boiled as our ranks were thinned and we saw death and dead everywhere and knew the Boche were still coming on to Bus and Barastre Villers and le Transloy, Lesboeufs, Bazentin, Martinpuich to Courcellette. We went backwards step by step. I see it all. At Courcellette we stayed a night, waiting orders which could not be given till it was known where our line ran and just how far the Germans had pushed. It was a ghastly night and I think most of us thought that by morning we should find ourselves surrounded. We got into action at Courcelette, and then went back to Miranmont, Thiepval, Aveluoy Wood and Mesnil – and still the Boche came on. He was drunk with success; we were exhausted with strain and the depression of it all. It is a nightmare to me still. Retreat is one of those events of life which can't be painted in too vivid words, and to which too strong adjectives cannot be applied.

Diary entries in 1918 record the end of the German offensive and our stand:

"March 30 Col F. B. Sykes took command of the Brigade. He has seen a lot of service and seems very businesslike. We shall get on well. I am still not feeling rested after the strain, responsibility, excitement and sleeplessness of these last few days which came before me with kaleidoscopic reality in my dreams. Every night I dream we are under orders to move suddenly." Other entries show the contradictions of that dreadful war – one day death and disaster, the next almost a summer holiday atmosphere.

"April 1: I am recommended today for the MC for my work. I wrote out all the other recommendations for the Brigade and saw my own.

"April 4: The Brigade went into action at Englebelmer. It rained all day. We are shelled out of Contay." At this time I learned that my father was dangerously ill. Leave was out of the question, of course, and I received the sad news of his death on April 23. Later I was sent home and got everything as straight as I could making arrangements for my mother to stay with relations for the time being. I returned to France with a sad heart, and on reaching Acheux found that our people had left. I tracked them down, to a nice camping ground near Varennes – where I had first joined the Division.

"May 12: It is lovely weather and bar an odd shell which fell very near my tent we had a comfortable time. I got up a sports meeting, with jumping competitions, mule and horse races."

Once the counter attack and advance started in June events moved even more rapidly than during the dreadful March

PLATE 1
The author in 1905, ready for a day with the Cleveland Hunt.

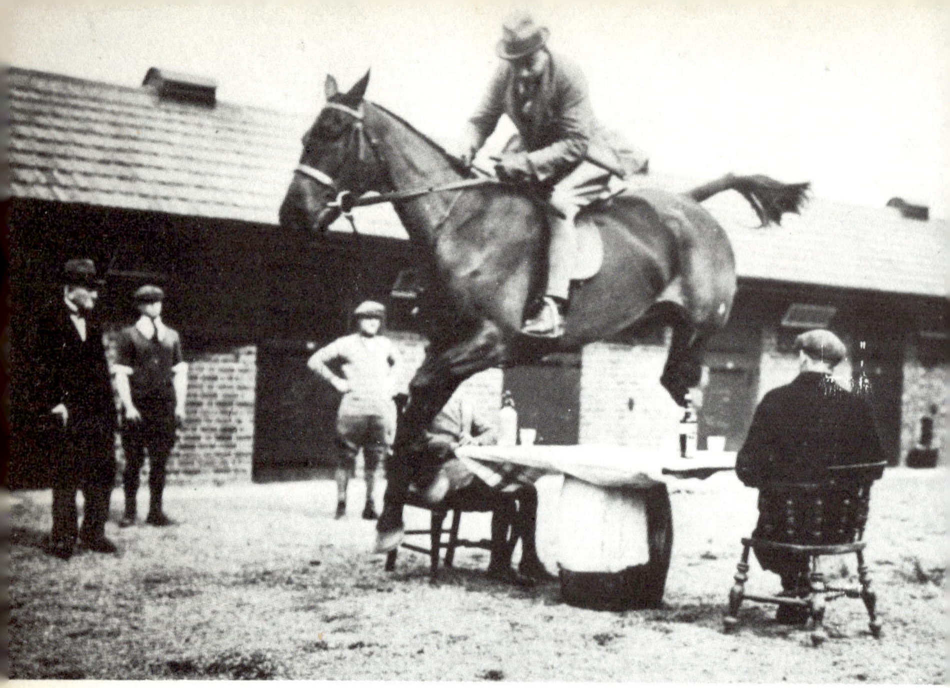

PLATE 2
At Hambleton in 1909 the author trick riding on John Dory.

PLATE 3
The author at Longmoor Barracks, Hampshire soon after being commissioned into the 15th (The King's) Hussars in 1914.

retreat. Our Brigade was quickly in action and the war was soon moving fast and furious. After leaving our base in a little village near Verdun we moved closer to the German border driving the Boche fast out of France. The battle was really hot and the Germans sent up observation balloons to try and spot our camouflaged guns. Even at this late stage, the pattern of the war was changing. Aeroplanes were becoming an ever increasing danger — bombing and machine gunning our lines. The Royal Flying Corps was playing a role of increasing importance too, and I saw a lot of dramatic air-fights, with the R.F.C. gallantly chasing and shooting down the Boche raiders. Our lines were shelled every two minutes, though, and machine gun fire marked every move that any of us made. We were so close to the Germans. As we advanced it was a case of moving from shell hole to shell hole.

I rode up to choose gun positions as near the front as possible. Things were very hot and the Germans could obviously see me. Suddenly gas shells began to explode and I was gassed. Later we went on to some gun positions and had to go full gallop part of the way because the Germans could see us — it was all rather like a nightmare foxhunt.

There was nothing left of Essart, when we reached the village. Snipers hid in the ruins, and the man beside me was killed by one of their bullets. I returned fire with my revolver and wounded and captured this German infantryman. He was only about 18 and looked even more frightened than I felt. My bullet had hit him in the shoulder, and he kept clutching at the wound and then drawing away his bloody hand with obvious terror.

Col. Sykes and I rode on to Ligny before it was clear of Boche. The village street was littered with the bodies of German soldiers and horses, and again snipers opened fire. Rounding-up the German stragglers was a quick job, and on we went to Riencourt and Bus. The Boche made a stand and our guns went into action with a fierce barrage — beating the enemy back again. The advance gained momentum.

During the second week in September Col. Sykes and I rode up to gun positions near Metz. Now we were only a few miles from Germany — and sensed victory. The advance went relentlessly on, all the while with a growing sense of triumph. We now enjoyed the comfort that the Boche had left a matter of minutes earlier. Their fires were still burning — and I half expected to find their cigarettes still smoking in the ash tins.

Soon we reached the wonderful Hindenberg line, a marvel of strength and defensive ingenuity. I had not long to study the maze of gun towers and tunnels, because we were advancing at speed, hindered only by the growing stream of German prisoners. Sometimes I rode 100 miles a day backwards and forwards looking for suitable positions to which our guns could advance. I had a fearsome ride one day, through a ravine lined with dead bodies. Shells were falling all around as I rode on but I found a suitable position for the guns, and a quarry that gave the horses shelter for their short rest.

One night Col. Sykes, the other officers and I had settled down to sleep when the Boche began to shell us like hell. One dropped into the farmyard where we had our horses — a few yards from the house — killing several. I got up and shouted through the window, smashed to smithereens by the shell, to see if the guard was alright. At that moment another shell burst just under the end of the house. The Colonel stuck his monocle in his eye, lit his pipe and began to look through his vest for lice singing "That will be glory for me." This broke the tension and made us laugh. Fritz put shells on each side of the house and we really thought our time had come and that the next shell would be a direct hit — but he switched off.

This was our last night in action and might well have been our last night on earth. Anyway next day we received orders to "pull out" for another front — we were on our way when Armistice was signed. The relief was boundless. At last this dreadful and hateful war was over. No one benefited. Everyone suffered — men, horses and mules. We all lost dear friends, and the tragedy of those years haunts me still. Also I am filled with horror and admiration when I think of the hundreds of horses under my command. Horror at their suffering and admiration at their continuing bravery, willingness and strength. The horse is a magnificent ally.

Never did I more admire the courage of the British Tommy than when each Christmas dawned. Many of those soldiers were little more than boys, but somehow they sang a song in a strange land; they created humour where no humour was, and they were firm in their resolve to maintain the old idea of Christmas even amid the comfortless, cold, mud and the certainty of uncertainty in France and Belgium. There was true heroism in all this. These boys swallowed the lumps in their throats, brushed aside the bitter disappointment that they were not amongst the lucky ones to get "Blighty" leave for Christmas. They resolved to help others — equally disappointed and longing for home, mother, family and friends — to find in their strangely contradictory surroundings, some of the love and merriment which is an integral part of the season.

I remember one Christmas my office was what had once been the potting shed in the garden of Equancourt chateau. The shed could accommodate only two or three people and outside stood a queue of the happiest lads in all the world. It was bitterly cold, the ground was frozen hard and the lads were weary, mud covered and nerved-strained; but they were going away from it all! They were going home! And so outside there was a joyous hum of voices as merry and carefree as those of a crowd of children waiting to go to the pantomime. Each man's warrant took some time to complete, but it came as a reprieve and so was well worth waiting for. All manner of details had to be filled in, certifying that the recipients had had baths and that clean, lice-free under-clothing had been supplied and so on. Very few of the lads had the chance of these luxuries, but who was going to queer their pitch of getting home for Christmas? Not me, and I doubt if any adjutant ever did. To each of them one wished a good time at home and the way their faces lighted up at the very mention of home was a tonic.

Awaiting the completion of a slip of paper in such circumstances, made the warrant precious beyond price, and endowed it with greater magic than any carpet in fairyland. As the last of the group saluted and filed away to lorry-jump or get as best they could to the railhead, there was a stinging sadness amongst those who were left. It was not mean envy of the temporary emancipation of others; not regret at being left behind with our hearts and thoughts somewhere in England. But a lump came into the throats of the bravest as they visualised the greetings awaiting the happy band of homeward bound pilgrims, when, in less than forty-eight hours they would re-join their family circles, often taking those at home by surprise.

And of those who remained. Well, as I have said our duty was not merely to keep a stiff upper lip, but to bring such happiness and laughter as we could to every man jack around us. To arrange, at any rate for those behind the lines, such entertainment and food as would bring something of the atmosphere of Christmas to all ranks. For a week or more before the great day, sacks containing the mail from home were so full and so increased in number that the little headquarter's cart could barely carry them. Folk at home were wonderfully generous, and determined that those overseas should not be without the cakes, plum puddings, mince pies and other fare inseparably associated with the season's festivities. And never did children await with more excitement and impatience the arrival of the postman during Christmas week. Never did youths and grown men of all ages and all ranks so unbend and for a brief while become their true selves. That which was truest and best came out in us, and our joy at remembrance was complete because we shared it in the spirit of brotherhood which alone sustained us in those days of danger, hardship, self-abnegation, yes, and fun too, when we had so much in common. It has been said that courage is the fear of being afraid, and it was with that sort of courage that many of us faced up to Christmastide, and ate, drank, laughed, sang and made merry. There were church services for those who were out of the line and at rest, and the padres did all they could to make the day a happy one. I think they succeeded too, and I remember one Christmas concert I attended in a hut in 1917, together with one amid the ruins of Arras, as being the best entertainments I enjoyed anywhere, before or since. How we all laughed, and with what self-abandon parties on their way back to billets in shacks, cow houses, stables, ruined barns and dug-outs sang "Good King Wenceslas." Sometimes it happened that when all arrangements had been made for Christmas Day in the rest area — which itself was often a sea of mud not far behind the firing line — the whole programme would be upset.

Those lads then laughed a hard laugh at their fate, and we in silent sympathy saw them march off into the night, up the road we knew so well, the road which was shelled by day and nights, the road up which the pack mules daily plodded with their burdens of ammunition. Urged on by their wonderful drivers, they hurried past certain dangerous points. Perhaps they, like us, breathed more freely when these particular "Hell-fire" corners were once more safely behind.

CHAPTER FIVE

JUDGING

When the war was over I got back to civilian life a wreck because I had not recovered from being gassed. I never have got over it and have difficulty in breathing every winter, even now. It was not easy to take up the threads again after such a long absence. I toyed with the idea of again becoming a trainer but soon realised that I had not the necessary capital to take stabling, buy saddlery and meet the wages and forage bills which would have to be paid for some time before any income was received. There were some influential and wealthy sportsmen who would have sent me horses – Jim Joel among them – but I could not bring myself to risk buying a training stable.

I left the army and returned to Grove House, Norton, near Stockton to take up the threads again. When my father died he had left many papers and manuscripts to be gone through and this, together with starting from scratch again, did not make rehabilitation any easier. In over four years I had lost touch, lost income and, after being in an expensive cavalry regiment, was more broke than usual.

I will never forget the kindness of Sir Alfred Pease. As soon as he heard that I was home he wired for me to lunch with him to discuss a private matter. He most generously offered an interest free loan until I got on my feet again. Much as I appreciated the offer I did not want to start on a loan, so I gratefully refused.

I started my racing articles again, and the now defunct *Empire News* and its sister paper the *Sporting Chronicle* took a series which brought me in £1,000. The *Sporting Chronicle* offered me the post of "Kettledrum" which meant writing a couple of columns a day, and giving tips. I have always avoided tipping in my sporting articles. As "Kettledrum" was expected to travel from race meeting to meeting, six days a week, and the salary was only about £1,000 a year I declined after going to Manchester for an interview.

Naturally, I had a desire for some peace and quiet and home-life, after nearly five years of squalor and war. By working seven days a week from 8 a.m. until 2 a.m. I was able to keep the bailiffs out of Grove House, where I was followed by the nuns attached to St. Mary's Catholic Church at Stockton. They had their own chapel in the roomy old house in which I wrote most of my 112 books. I knew the Reverend Mother and most of the nuns for, on my return to civilian life, I again began to serve first Mass — which they attended — at St. Mary's every morning when I was at home.

I had not long been home before W. J. Trenholme, clerk of the course at Sedgefield, asked me if I would judge at the next meeting. A number of members of the National Hunt Committee were intimate friends of mine and, of course, I knew all those controlling Jockey Club and National Hunt affairs at Messrs. Weatherbys, so had no difficulty in getting a licence.

Naturally I was very nervous when I reported for my first afternoon's duty as a Judge in 1919. The responsibilities of a Judge are onerous, and the consequent pressures are very considerable. These are obviously magnified in every Judge's novice days. I was certainly no exception, and was shaking rather as I climbed into the Judge's box for the first race.

The Sedgefield course is narrow and on that cold winter's day in 1919 there were 23 hurdlers in the line-up for the first race. About eight of them finished in a bunch. There was dead silence in the stands after this thrilling finish. The silence was broken when the numbers went up. A punter with a stentorian voice shouted, "He isn't fit to judge a donkey race on Redcar sands." That was a verdict not calculated to give me the greatests encouragement and confidence!

No matter how long a man may have been going racing, or how familiar he is with most owners' colours and the peculiarities of certain jockeys — often so helpful to judges — it does require confidence and ability, quick sight and decision, to pick out the first four horses from a big field, and also assess the distances separating them.

Even though my entry into the ranks of Turf officialdom may not have been popularly acclaimed by all, I was quite sure that my decision was right so was not unduly disturbed by the outspoken criticism. Indeed the shout served to boost my confidence. I was so sure of my own correct judgement that I at once gained complete indifference to any uproar from amateurs in the stands who were doubtless shouting through their pockets anyway.

Not all the criticism came from thwarted punters, of course. On this same Springfield course my old friend the late Capt. Jim Storie swore I had cheated him out of a race. I gave a short head verdict against him when he rode Frizbury owned by Brig.-Gen. Rotton. But Jim was as nice as could be about it, so was General Rotton, though the latter afterwards always referred to me as "the unjust judge". As a matter of fact Jim was "pipped" on the post just as I saw him "pip" Capt. Percy Bewicke at Hexham years before.

As soon as the *Racing Calendar* published the news that I had been granted a Judge's licence, Brigadier General Sir Loftus Bates asked me to judge at Hexham, Rothbury, Carlisle, Kelso, Perth, Catterick and the other meetings that he controlled. This was a wonderful appointment, and founded a close liaison with Sir Loftus that was to span almost 30 years.

I suppose all those who have held the office of Judge — even since the days of photo-finish — have made mistakes, though not so many as some members of the public would make out. In a close finish only those absolutely in a line with the winning post can pretend to know who has won. As Jack Colling often remarked to me "You never know what's won until the numbers go up . . . and not always then." One of the most glaring errors I ever saw made by a judge was at Thirsk in 1911 when the late "Piggy" Finlay was officiating. The mistake was all the more remarkable in view of the fact that there was not a close finish in the race and that there was no similarity in the colours. It was after the White Mare Plate for two-year-olds that Finlay joisted the number of W. Wilson's Ask Papa (H. Randall), as the winner with Compton Vyner's Formamint (W. Bullock), second, the official distance being "half-a-length". Actually Formamint (second favourite), had won by nearly two lengths.

Mr. Vyner was a steward at the meeting, and he, like everyone else, was astounded. The crowd showed their disagreement in a frightening way not often heard on a racecourse. I can remember. Billy Bullock getting into the scale as the winner and refusing to believe Jack Atkinson, clerk of the scales, who said that he was second. Randall announced, "I was beaten by more than a length," to which Atkinson replied: "The judge evidently doesn't think so!" Mr. Vyner's face muscles were twitching with exasperation and annoyance as he stood in the weighing-room. The other stewards approached the judge to ask if he was quite satisfied with his decision, and, despite the pandemonium outside, Finlay insisted that he was right. The wrong verdict stood. From what he told me afterwards the Thirsk incident must have preyed on Finlay's mind for he said he frequently dreamed the race over again and always saw Ask Papa as the winner. Billy Bullock never referred to winning the 1908 Derby and Oaks on Signorinetta, but always he asked: "Do you remember the Ask Papa and Formamint race at Thirsk?"

Billy did once recall his classic triumphs when he asked me to contradict a statement in a national paper that the Italian trainer had given him £1,000 as a present. What Bullock actually received was a glass of wine and a cigar. That reminds me that after winning a little race for me I once told that great jockey George McCall, that I was a poor man and could not afford more than "a pony" as a present. The reply was "Often I don't even get 'Thank you!'"

I remember Billy Hammet having a bad fall at Carlisle when riding a heavily-backed hot-pot. Despite a lip cut in two Hammett remounted and won the race. The owner appeared most grateful after fearing that his bets were down the drain. But he showed his gratitude by buying Hammett only a packet of twenty cigarettes! As the disgusted jockey's lip needed a lot of stitches he could not even smoke those.

Carlisle reminds me of an incident on that course when I was judging. After a close finish I gave a decision which was very unpopular. About a dozen of "the boys" made for me in an excited and threatening state of mind. Standing at one side of my box during the race was Dan Sutherland who worked commissions for some stables and on the other side was Bill Percival. He was a cattle dealer, a considerable landowner, and the confidant of Dobson Peacock, for whose Middleham stable he acted in the ring when they had anything worth backing. When the toughs menacingly demanded that I should reverse the placings of the first and second, Sutherland, who was well-known to them as pretty useful with his fists, addressed them: "Don't talk so daft! I was standing in a line with the winning-post and had a monkey on the second, but before the numbers went up I knew I'd lost my money." "And I'd backed the second," added Bill Percival, "but the judge's placings are right." They saved the situation and I was grateful as I hurried away to the weighing room.

Bill Percival was responsible for the much-liked Charlie Jackson, of Darlington, dabbling in real estate very successfully. Charlie is an old friend of mine, who has bred bloodstock and had horses in training for a long time. He won the Cumberland Plate and Goodwood Stakes in 1933 with Prince Oxendon.

I remember once judging at Bogside on a wild, wet day in 1921 when the colours were so soaked they all looked alike, number cloths were blown up and jockeys, unrecognisably mud-bespattered, lost their caps in the gale. There were a lot of runners in one race and, having nothing to help me to place the first four horses, "Ginger" Firth, who was a starter, and afterwards clerk of course at York, asked if he could be of any help in picking me the third and fourth. He recognised how difficult was the task of a judge under the prevailing conditions and I gladly accepted his kindly offer. I got what I thought were the first and second and asked Firth what he made third. When he gave me the number I checked in my judge's book and said: "Well! that one didn't even start!" I had to wait at the scale till the rider claiming to be third came to weigh in before I could have his number put in the frame on trust.

On another occasion, at the sporting little Rothbury meeting in 1923 there was an amateur race in which a number of sporting farmers rode. Four or five of them all had dark blue jerseys with differentiating caps. As the first three all lost their caps and their number-cloths were hidden by their saddles I had no means of identifying them at all. I ran to the gate through which the horses returned to the paddock and asked the two I recognised as first and second — the third was on a grey so I had got him — what they were riding. It was some time before I could get anything more out of the winner than that he intended "te lay a hobjection". I kept assuring him he had won and after some delay the numbers went up.

At Hexham in 1927 the man with me at the judge's box to put the numbers up there, spoke broad Northumbrian and expected I did the same. When I told him 14 was the winner, he put 13 in the frame. A yell from the crowd called my attention to the error and when I told him 14 had won, he replied: "Thorteen is in the frame." My 14 and his "thorteen" evidently sounded the same to him.

At Perth the same year I caused another rumpus by putting up the "first three" numbers in the frame before the race was over. There was a mistake on the card as to the distance and I remarked to Capt. Tommy Henderson, who was standing by my box, "That was a queer sort of finish — it looked as though none of them were very busy." Then we both saw that the race was still in progress.

I used to enjoy judging at the most sporting little Brocklesby meeting in Lincolnshire and was sorry when it was dropped. On the first occasion I acted there I was told that I had been appointed because the previous judge had nearly caused a riot by trying to satisfy and placate the crowd. They booed when he gave his first verdict in a race, so he had the numbers taken down and transposed the order of 1 and 2. As this brought louder boos, he altered his decision to a dead-heat. Quite a man to follow!

At one time four or five men acted together as "triers" — the early name for judge — and afterwards, when it became a one-man job, they didn't seem very particular who was appointed at little country meetings.

Stokesley race meeting ceased as a flat race fixture in 1874 owing to the new Jockey Club rule that no meeting would be recognised unless at least £300 was given as added money for each day's racing and no race was worth less than £100. There was, however, a National Hunt fixture at Stokesley until 1881. The final winner was ridden by Bob Adams on View Holloa, carrying 13st. 3lb. He had won the first race on the same horse. Squire Abington Baird also rode a winner at this closing down fixture, at which four races had £20 added and two had £22 added money.

Francis "Franky" Hunter started life as a barber in Stockton but gave up business after winning a lot of money over one of the classics. He then devoted his life to sport and was often asked to judge at Stokesley. I never saw him, or his contemporary George Hodgson, in any other head-dress than a silk-hat. Hunter died a very old man in the early 1900s. He had been a member of Stockton Race Committee and was one of those responsible for the revival of Stockton races in 1855. He and Thomas Parrington — who was born at Middlesbrough when his father's farm and labourers' cottages were the only houses there – saw the possibilities of Mandale Bottoms as a racecourse. I had it from Mr. Parrington's own lips that he called a meeting in 1854 at the Black Lion Hotel at Stockton and with Dr. W. Richardson, J. S. Sutton, Harry Fowler, Frank Hunter and Jos Dodds, formed themselves into a committee. They appointed Thomas Craggs, who lived in Bishopton-lane, Stockton as clerk of the course. It is interesting to add that Mr. Parrington as Master of the Sinnington Hounds was the first to arrange a hound show – held on the racecourse at Redcar – and the first to organise a class for thoroughbred stallions.

Brocklesby, at which I judged for some years, was the only meeting I know of at which all the officials wore badges like those on the coats of the judges, committeemen, secretary and president at agricultural shows. They were similar to those displayed by bookmakers who are members of the BPA. At Brocklesby the Bishop of Lincoln evidently thought I didn't look like a welsher for he asked me the price for some runner. I replied that I hadn't the foggiest idea. He then said: "But you are a bookmaker, aren't you?"

I gave up judging because of a rather outspoken novel – one of the thirteen I published in one year – which put me under a cloud with the Jockey Club. On reflection the whole episode seems remarkably silly, almost unbelievable. At the end of 1934 my Judge's licence was not renewed immediately on the usual application. Asking the reason I discovered that I was being treated like a naughty boy because I had dared to criticise the almighty Jockey Club in my novel *Warned Off*. Indeed I was being put in the corner for a time. I was told that as a racecourse official I should not write Turf novels and that I was under the "pained displeasure" of the Jockey Club. I approached one of the Stewards, who informed me that I would be required to appear before the Stewards presumably to give an undertaking that I would not write anything about the inner workings of racing again. Before I was summoned to appear, the licence arrived. Now it was my turn to be rash and hasty. In pique I returned the licence saying that I refused to have any curb — real or implied — placed on my work as an author or journalist. The cause of all this personal furore was inspired by the unjust timelessness of the "warned off" sentence.

Warned Off criticised the Jockey Club for not stating a definite period for the "warning off". The inspiration was Jim Adams. The criticism was gentle but I have always felt that it was most unfair that a trainer or jockey should lose his licence not knowing when, if ever, he would get it back. A Judge cannot just send a man to prison. The term of the sentence must be stated — a week, a month, a year or life. The Jockey Club should always have acted in the same way. Now they do so — but this change of heart came more than 30 years after my novel. I sought the "definite sentence" so that a man would know whether to hold on to his Turf connections in the hope that the licence would be returned in one, two or three years; or whether he should seek other employment knowing that he was finished in racing for life. This seemed only fair to me — but the result was the loss of my licence as a racecourse judge. The novel told the story of an experienced jockey who let a beautiful and persuasive girl talk him into throwing away a race so that her lover could land a gambling coup and clear his debts. Thickening the plot I introduced "murder" and made the girl the daughter of Senior Steward of the Jockey Club, Lord Farndale. The passage that the Jockey Club objected to was that describing the jockey's feelings after losing his licence:

"Saddened and miserable as he was and anxious to get away from London as quickly as possible, he had no feeling of grievance against the Jockey Club, except that in doing what he had expected of them their sentence was indefinite. As in the case of others who are similarly punished by the governing body of the Turf for serious breaches of the moral laws of racing, there was hope left for reinstatement, but no hint as to when. The sentence might be for one year, two years, five or ten. It might even be for life, as in the case of Tod Sloan. Year by year he applied for his licence, only to receive the usual brief acknowledgement and the equally brief announcement that it had not been granted. He and others have refrained from endeavouring to take up some other means of livelihood and have continued to keep themselves fit in the expectation that they would be back in the saddle next season. But in some cases the next season, and the one after that, and others come and go, till those who wait lose hope and know that it is too late even if they were forgiven and granted a licence to ride. In his autobiography Tod Sloan says that when his licence was refused him he 'could not bring myself to believe that they would keep me out all the season. If I had known then what I learnt in after years, that my indiscretions were to be reckoned against me for half some people's lifetime, the whole course of my life and investments would have been different. With £60,000 odd and other property I might have done really well. I was only twenty-seven years old and was sure I could ride as well or better than ever. The majority of my friends stuck to me through all this and cheered me more than can be said. But they were not happy days. The more inquiries were made as to the possibility of getting my ticket back again the more undecided seemed the situation. It was a sickening business, too, when in London having to reply to all sorts of people — some of whom I had scarcely ever met — as to what I was going to do. The truth was I didn't know. The number of nights which were spent on trying to make up my mind I can't count, but plans made whilst lying awake were quite upset by a few words of encouragement the next day given by serious friends who knew, I supposed, what they were talking about. What with hope and fear in 1902 I was going through Hell.'

"That was precisely what Tom Jewison felt as he drove along the Great North Road towards Doncaster. The whole world for him seemed turned backwards. He knew nothing but racing, had been amongst horses ever since he left school, and had no other interests. His size and weight precluded him from following any other occupation if the Jockey Club treated him as they had done Tod Sloan. He alternately feared they would, and cheered himself with the thought that he might only have to stand down till the end of the season. Even so, what was he to do with himself till then? He had always heard that those who had incurred the displeasure of the Jockey Club were advised to sink themselves in oblivion, to be neither seen nor heard of till the cloud was lifted."

Later in the novel my character Lord Farndale was to say: "If I had my way men like Jewison would not only be warned off for life, but their cases would be placed before the Public Prosecutor so that he could institute civil proceedings and have such blackguards sent to penal servitude together with all their accomplices. No matter who they were I'd have the law set on the whole bag of tricks of them."

There was, of course, a happy ending. Lord Farndale's daughter confessed. Jewison was granted permission to work in racing stables, and told that his licence would be renewed.

So ended that part of my Turf career, even though my Judge's licence was renewed I had rejected it. A man needs to be very fit and well, full of confidence, quick of sight and action, and with the skin of a rhinoceros, to be a judge. Even then it can become a strain. I later acted as starter, as clerk-of-scales, stakeholder, assistant clerk of the course and as club secretary at several meetings. As a matter of fact, except for making a book and acting as handicapper, I have done everything on a racecourse. If I had carried out the wishes of Sir Loftus Bates I should have taken out a licence as a handicapper. I declined, knowing that I had too sensitive a temperament to stand being continually tackled by owners and trainers with complaints that their horses had been unfairly treated. More than once I have known owners take the handicapper before Stewards to explain why their horses have been given burdens — they said — far greater than their public form warranted. On several occasions the same horses have won despite the weight complained of! Handicappers sometimes take note of things not recorded in the form book.

PLATE 4
Judging at Sedgefield Races in 1920, the author with *(from left to right)* W. Trenholme (Clerk of the Course), Bob Trenholme (Clerk of Scales) and Bob Harper (Starter).

PLATE 5
The author talks to Bob Armstrong at Catterick in 1928.

PLATE 6
Hewitt Henry Golightly and Sir Gordon Richards.

Sir Loftus, who had given my career as a judge such a boost in 1919, came to my rescue against sixteen years later when I rejected my licence. By this time he was becoming increasingly troubled with deafness, and employed me to relieve him of his many responsibilities at Thirsk, Hamilton Park, Lanark and Pontefract. He generously acknowledged all the help I gave him in the introduction he wrote for one of my Turf books.

Sir Loftus had about a dozen meetings to supervise and I assisted him at all of them working as clerk-of-scales, supervising the declarations of runners and generally acting as assistant clerk of all the courses, from 1935 onwards. When he retired from Pontefract I was asked to succeed him. Doubtless other meetings would in due course have been offered me but, apart from the knowledge that the Pontefract directorate was very difficult to deal with, the business side of racing never appealed to me and I declined.

Years before I had turned down a similar offer from Bob Thornton, who farmed near Darlington and usually had a point-to-pointer and 'chaser in training. I saw him at most northern race meeting and he evolved a scheme for laying down a track by the side of the River Tees near where Sir Henry Havelock-Allan lived. So enthusiastic was he, and so persistent, that I got Miles I'Anson to have a look at the proposed new course. This would be about 1910, when I'Anson managed most of the racecourses between Doncaster and Scotland. The three of us went to see the prospective track which had great possibilities as a racecourse, but I'Anson's verdict was "There is no chance of making a race meeting here pay. Catterick, an old established fixture, barely pays its way, and I don't suppose the Jockey Club would grant a licence to another track so near at hand."

Working for Sir Loftus was always interesting and varied. There were additional duties — including the issue of free luncheon and tea tickets and complimentary badges to owners, trainers and others, who for one reason or another, are admitted to racecourses without payment. The number who try to obtain their racing without cost is astounding. The duties of a club secretary require an intimate knowledge of the great racing public and of the importuning, shameless, "dead-heads" who year by year are bent on — and often succeed in — getting their racing for nothing. Recognising them and an ability to diagnose human nature and to determine when a man is "telling the tale", impersonating and so on, is essential to be able to do one's duty to save race executives hundreds of pounds a year. Even when I had refused some of these dead-heads free entry, I sometimes found them in the club wearing a complimentary badge which they had persuaded some owner or trainer to get for them. They hang about outside after being told they would have to pay and spot someone, as mean as themselves, about to enter the club office. "As you have no one with you, get the two badges you are allowed and give me one," is the request of the dead-head. I think I did a lot to stop this traffic. Anyhow I was plainly told by one of the non-paying fraternity: "You are the most unpopular Turf official in England! Your name stinks in nostrils of 'the regulars'."

Make no mistake, race officialdom is a strenuous and exhausting business necessitating long journeys and much highly concentrated work crowded into a few hours, starting long before racing begins. Then another long journey, when one is tired, to some other racecourse to begin all over again. Many think of the Scottish circuit as a delightful holiday. I went the round of the meetings over the borders for many years but was not one who looked on it as anything but very hard work. It meant being away from home too long. In addition, unlike most of the "regulars" I always had many hours of work to do in the evening. Often I had the race card for the following day to compile and to see through the printers, and then had to write, or type, the twenty-odd columns of newspaper matter I write each week. I remember at one Scottish meeting I judged, did the declarations, issued badges and luncheon tickets, acted as weighing-room liaison officer for the Tote and attended to all the stake-holder's considerable duties — receiving entry and jockeys' fee, insurance, and forfeits, due to other meetings.

In Scotland I had many good friends some of whom kindly invited me to stay with them for their local race meeting. Once or twice I was the guest of Lord Hamilton of Dalzell, who was such a success when Senior Jockey Club Steward and was largely responsible for the introduction of the Tote into this country. I also stayed with Robertson Aikman at The Ross, near Hamilton Park, where, as at Lanark, he acted as Steward.

At Ayr races I always spent an evening with the late Johnny McGuigan, who trained there and exported a lot of bloodstock. Shortly before his death I edited his memoirs. He attended every north country meeting and his son Davy was for years one of the best-known jockeys in the North.

But being one of a house party does not fit in with race officialdom, especially when, as in my case, one has much literary work to do and possibly 30 or 40 letters to answer. This made it impossible to enter into the social life of the fellow guests. So latterly, I declined all invitations finding hotels left me much more a free agent.

At the start of the Second World War in 1939 I volunteered for Army Service. I suppose I was dreaming to think that the Army would want a 56-year-old veteran, but I hoped that there might be some job for me. Of course my application was rejected but I was offered duty as a Manpower Board official. Thinking that I must do my bit I took this post — and from the start hated every second of my work. The Manpower Board had to check the authenticity of the reasons for exemption given by those called up for the Forces. This meant trailing round factories and questioning people as though they were all frightened shirkers. I stuck it for a while, but then resigned. Although there was racing work for me only at Pontefract for several years, I was very busy writing books and articles. My wife Doris trained as a St. John's Ambulance nurse, and we opened the large cellar of Grove House as an air-raid shelter. I waited anxiously for the six o'clock news every day — full of concern for our soldiers, airmen and sailors going through the same hell that we had all come to dread some 25 years earlier.

Doris and I moved from Grove House to remote Westerdale near Whitby, Yorkshire in 1945. This made travel to race-meetings hard because I never have driven a car. Nevertheless the peace, and the tranquillity of our new home made all the difficulties worth while. Low House was built in 1673 and over the door are the words "My lot is in a fair place, and a goodly heritage." Here there is love, peace, quiet, content and inspiring beauty on every hand.

I love Low House and towards the end of my days as a race-course official, hated the time spent away from its thick comforting stone walls and warmth.

I first went racing at Thirsk in 1902 little thinking that I would later become an official there. But such I was for many years. I retired in 1958 feeling that I had been rather shabbily treated, though now that the wound has healed I realise that Col. Johnny Johnson, who was clerk of the course — and who acknowledged in letters that "I had put him in the saddle at Thirsk" — felt that at well over 70 I was due to join the hallelujah chorus rather than take new Turf appointments. For nearly 40 years I was general "stooge" at Thirsk races at a fee little higher than that of a gateman. At the latter end of those years Sir Loftus Bates was clerk of the course and he left more and more of the work to me. Before the advent of stewards' secretaries and official shorthand writers, I marshalled those the stewards wished to interview, took a shorthand note of questions and replies and wrote the official statement regarding their inquiries for *The Racing Calendar*. Often I undertook the compilation of the race card. I had the issuing of complimentary badges, lunch and tea tickets and when the totalisator brought about the compulsory declaration of runners, I was deputed to receive these and draw up lists before each race for officials and number-boards.

All this made me one of the busiest men on the course from a couple of hours before racing commenced until after the last event. The duty meant non-stop concentration. I often dealt with about 300 people and was interrupted by having to leave my office to answer telephone calls in the clerk of the course's room and by trainers wishing me to find them a jockey. After a particularly hectic day at Thirsk in 1957, with big fields, withdrawals of horses, changes of jockeys, more than the usual number of disgruntled – some abusive – importuners for badges and free meals I had a seizure. One side of my body was affected and I had difficulty in getting into a car which was to take me home. I did not work for several days but with the aid of a stick I went to Redcar Races the following week, saw the red light and decided that if I was to continue my long connection with Thirsk Races it must be in a less strenuous capacity.

At that time my old friend Nat Allgood – cousin of Miss Clayton and her trainer brother Jack – had a fatal seizure while out grouse shooting with Lord Allendale. He was club secretary at Thirsk, Catterick, Newcastle and Carlisle and I thought his Thirsk job would provide the easier post I wanted. It was one for which I was very fitted with my knowledge of the racing fraternity. I told Col. Johnson, Lord Middleton and Major Gordon Foster – directors of the race company – that I would like the post but Col. Johnson wanted it for a friend of his and thought it would be unwise to appoint someone as old as myself. I was very hurt at the time despite the nice letters I had from Gordon Foster and Lord Middleton and their invitation to their private boxes and to lunch in the stewards' room whenever I cared to go to Thirsk Races.

I carried on as club secretary at Redcar and as clerk of scales at Catterick until 1961 and then retired completely from racecourse duty. This was a wrench, but as owner, trainer and jockey, judge and official, I had then completed some 65 active years on the Turf. And I had enjoyed nearly every minute of that time.

CHAPTER SIX

GANGSTERS

"'The Birmingham Boys' are on the train" or "at the meeting." This warning, passed from racecourse regular to racecourse regular, prompted immediate – and justified – fear. The Birmingham Boys were a gang of real rough, tough and merciless desperados. They operated mainly on the Midlands and Northern courses and made rich pickings on the race trains. In the late 1800's and the years before the First World War nearly all punters travelled from course to course by train – often with their pockets full of money. The Birmingham Boys aimed, one way or another, to get that money, either on the way to the race meeting or on the homeward journey. Hopeful gentlemen aiming to beat the bookmakers, their wallets bulging with ready cash were their "pigeons" while successful backers happily returning with bookmakers cash were "sitting ducks".

The ringleaders of the gang were known to most regular racegoers and, of course, to the local police, though not to the constables drafted from country districts on to racecourses. In those days there was no regular Turf staff of Ring Inspectors. Time after time it was thought that the gang had been broken up, but it was reformed with new and virile brains to govern and direct operations. So the robbery continued, often with violence. Sometimes the gang used mere pickpocket tricks and occasionally more carefully thought out schemes were operated all devoted to relieving others of their money, although The Birmingham Boys never really had a master mind capable of engineering anything really original in the way of crime. They relied more upon quickness, violence, brute strength, terrorism and their reputation for revenge.

Unless they had some individual marked down as prey they did not often travel the Scottish Racing Circuit. Perhaps this was because there was a rival gang in Glasgow and that a certain honour existed between thieves in recognising each other's territory. The Glasgow Boys were even more crude in their methods than those from Birmingham. They were much less skilful than the Midlanders and relied less upon pocket-tapping, than upon blackmail with threats of, and actual, violence to those bookmakers and backers who did not part with money or have ex-pugulists by their sides as protection. A favourite plan of the Glasgow gang was to collect for a bogus mine charity. Those bookmakers who failed to contribute, and contribute handsomely, knew that it was likely that the money would be taken from them, or that they would not be allowed to stand up and bet.

There was yet another gang of "boys" who went on tour to race meetings and coursing fixtures. They hailed from Mexborough — each "gang" taking the name of its home town — and occasionally fell foul of the Birmingham roughs with the result that there were free fights and sometimes "peachings" to the police. The recriminations on such occasions were often desperate and bloody. Of the three well-known bands the one from Birmingham was the most notorious. It was largely through their activities that so many bookmakers found it necessary to have a bruiser or two always by their side when betting and travelling on race trains.

I knew for a fact that there was a good deal of collusion between the police and the Birmingham brigade. I have myself seen local police at race meetings not only accept bribes but give the hint to others that there was "money for nothing" if they walked past individuals and stared hard at them. It was the same on race trains. Occasionally someone came along to each carriage and called out "card-sharpers are on the train" but a few pound notes distributed to officials and police often resulted in the three-card gentry travelling without hindrance, plundering those fools who were vain enough to think they could get the best of the battle of wits and sleight of hand. I often thought that the accomplices acted better than anyone I have ever seen on the stage. A card sharp once told me they rehearsed their novices for weeks at a little Birmingham club before they were allowed to take the part of the successful "Lady Spotter" — who apparently won and was paid a good deal of money before others in the carriage were invited to join in and be robbed. Then there was the kindly stranger who turned up the corner of the winning cards when the dealer's attention was apparently diverted. Of course he dealt again and somehow managed to turn up another card. There was a good deal of acquired skill in the manipulations of the cards, but still more, at least so it always struck me, in selecting likely victims. The cheats must have had wonderful intuitive knowledge of character and human nature, as well as remarkable memories for faces. They appeared to know all those whose business took them racing regularly and never seemed to expect them to have a flutter. What they did expect, and sometimes openly requested, was that those "in the know," would not, what they termed "spoil the fun."

I never had much sympathy with those who lost money to "the Boys" at the three-card or similar tricks. They were running their heads into a noose with their eyes wide open, actuated by pure greed. But, profitable as this side line of the Birmingham Boys often was, it was not their main business. Picking pockets, hanging round bookies to see who was paid out large sums, or backing something heavily, then altering the numbers of betting tickets and getting in first to draw when the horse had won, were amongst their main activities. They would carefully note where a successful backer stored away his money, and would shadow him all day to obtain a favourable opportunity to relieve him of his winnings. If that opportunity did not come either in the stands, in the paddock, or as the victim left the course, some of the gang would follow him to the railway station and travel with him to wait their chance. They would follow their victim to his hotel and even go up in the lift with him if they did not discover the number of his room in the entrance hall. They were as persistent and relentless as a stoat after a rabbit, and often as successful.

I remember Bob Robson telling me how he and a Newmarket trainer had had a very successful time at Worcester with their horses. They were betting in "ready" and had hundreds of pounds in their pockets. They had adjoining rooms and on returning to their hotel from the course went straight upstairs to wash. Bob went to his companion's room to suggest that they put their money into the hotel safe. He was discussing the matter when three of the Birmingham gang entered and shut the door.

"You know what we've come for!" briefly announced one of them, adding "and we mean to have it." It was three against two, but the trainers were both men who could use their fists and who were not easily cowed. Without a moment's hesitation Bob picked up a chair and broke it over the head of one of the Birmingham boys. He dropped like a log and a desperate fight between the other two began. It was strange that despite the crashing windows and shouts not a soul in the hotel arrived on the scene. Perhaps other guests heard the din but not knowing who were the attacked or attackers, thought they were wisest out of a race row. Eventually the trainers got the better of their men, who then made a dash for the door, got it open and fled down the corridor. The one who had been knocked out scrambled to his feet and managed to escape too. None of the trio put in an appearance at the races on the following day, or arrest would certainly have followed.

There was at one time cause for real fear if anyone did give any of the gang away to the police. One man whose body was mysteriously discovered on a railway line, and another who was found unconscious in a train corridor, with his head split by a broken bottle, were both believed to have been marked down by members of the Birmingham gang for having been instrumental in the arrest of some of their members. I remember once asking a well known bookmaker, who had been held up and compelled to part with a considerable sum of money, why he didn't have the men arrested. He knew them well by sight and could easily have pointed them out to the police. He replied: "It would be as much as my life was worth. That gang never forget and never forgive. They would wait for years to get their own back but sooner or later they would be revenged. They are like one of those foreign secret societies which form a vendetta and will strike a man in the back, in the dark – anywhere – so long as they get what they consider satisfaction."

They were not cowards, however un-English their methods very often were, and the daring impertinence of some of their schemes filled us with wonder. Trading on their reputation they never worked singly and it is probable that this gave them an added confidence. I remember on one occasion a plain clothes detective telling me he had watched the Birmingham gang working the buses outside the paddock gates at Carlisle in 1908. They adopted the old plan of attempting to force their way through a crowd as though trying to make sure of a seat, and made a real good haul of pocket-books and wallets. The detective could do nothing single handed but the following day had a number of police watching. Not one of the "Boys" was there. They had probably taken several hundred pounds the previous day and were not only satisfied but guessed there would be a strong contingent of local police waiting for them on the following afternoon if they attempted to repeat their performance.

On another occasion they descended on Ripon races and some days later a farmer four miles out of Ripon on the Harrogate road found a collection of nearly fifty wallets, purses and pocket books behind a hedge in one of his fields. There were also some cheap watches which the gang knew it was useless taking to the melting pot of their Birmingham receiver. The gang were careful not to retain anything valuable which would give them away. Many a treasured heirloom, trinket, watch, pin and cigarette case for the return of which the owner would gladly have paid a hundred times its value and made no enquiry, could not be returned because it had gone into the pot the same evening. The receiver's pot was kept going day and night and the only chance of retrieving stolen property was to get in touch with some of the gang before they left the race course.

Lord Lonsdale told me with delight the story of how he once got a watch back and, I fancy, an apology from the head of the Birmingham Boys who explained that it was a new hand who had gone through his Lordship's pockets without knowing who he was.

That famous Turfite Sir John Astley, known to all and sundry as "The Mate" had a similar meeting with the gang when at Epsom on City and Suburban day. Sir John felt his watch being removed from his pocket and saw it passed to another man, whom he then seized. There was a scrimmage but Sir John stuck to his man until the police came. The detectives told him that they had never before known anything recovered once a pickpocket had passed it to a confederate.

Only once in their long history of blackmail, violence, robbery, assault and crime generally, were the Birmingham Boys really routed. That was when Lord Marcus Beresford and a number of other gentlemen, who made no secret of their liking for a scrap stood up to them and gave them a sound thrashing. This happened at Shrewsbury in 1878 when a number of Lord Beresford's pals were present accompanied by several of their friends – most of whom had passed through one or the other of schools of pugilism then conducted by popular ex-fighting men.

At the time John Frail, who was clerk of the course and manager of the Shrewsbury race fixture for 50 years, was also Mayor of the town. This was five years before I was born, but the legend of the Shrewsbury race gang rout was repeated with delight at every Turf gathering in my early racing days – when the fear of the race gangs was still ever present.

The Shrewsbury meeting opened on Tuesday, November 12th, 1878 and among those present were the Duke of Montrose, Lord Marcus, Sir John Astley, Capt. Hartopp and Sir T. Hesketh. Not a favourite won, and the bookmakers in the ring had a good time. "Outside" some of the layers who had offered tremendous odds, welshed when the long-priced horses won. They were caught, stripped and badly mauled. The police were powerless and no one else was inclined to raise a finger to help them. Indeed the crowd rather enjoyed the fun and joined in the hunt and the battery. Probably the Birmingham Boys had nothing at all to do with these disturbances, which were not uncommon in the free, or cheap parts of racecourses at this period. The Birmingham Boys were far too wide awake when having a wager, to entrust their money to anyone shouting over the odds. They knew every sound penciller, and all those who fully intended to leave their stands and run if they saw by the progress of the race it was likely they were going to have to pay out.

What the Birmingham Boys did know was that the bookmakers of substance and reputation in Tattersall's had had a very successful afternoon and must be in possession of considerable sums of money. Also they wanted revenge on Ex-Sgt. Ham, who had retired from the detective force and was employed by the clerks of various courses to keep out of paddocks those whom he knew to be undesirable. Ham had stood at the pay-gate to the Shrewsbury paddock and told the men in charge not to admit any gang members. Afterwards he had others "known to the police" turned out of the paddock just before the first race. How they got in was a mystery until later one of them was seen attempting to return by climbing from the track into the judge's box.

The aim of the riot at Shrewsbury races was to murder Sgt. Ham and take toll of the bookmakers afterwards. The ex-detective was not only a man of tremendous courage but also possessed much experience of thieves and other criminals. Moreover he was absolutely straight and "unbuyable". He never threw any chances away, and always said he had eyes at the back of his head. Sgt. Ham, knowing what strong men Lord Marcus Beresford and Capt. "Chicken" Hartopp were confided in them. Ham reported that the gang planned to attack him as he left the racecourse. "Those Birmingham Boys have sworn to do me in," he said "and they hate me more than ever after I've kept them out of the paddock this afternoon. There threatens to be a dangerous disturbance."

"If there's to be trouble we'll be there" promised Lord Marcus, who added "but the few police there are here would be worse than useless if those Birmingham fellows mean business. The Boys would laugh at them. You can rely on me and my pals and so long as they'll fight with their fists I'll back my friends and myself to be good enough. It's knives and bottles that I can't stand in a fight, but in any case we will do our utmost to see that you are safe and that other racegoers are not harmed."

Frail had also become anxious. Racecourse rows were not uncommon but he knew that the very scum of Birmingham Turf rogues were present. Ham had told him that he had had at least thirty turned away from the paddock gates at which they had — having failed to find a means of "gate grashing" or free entrance — tendered payment. Apart from the fact that they did not come to a meeting for nothing Frail knew that they were thoroughly roused and determined to get their own back, for the indignity they had received. So in the middle of the afternoon he sent a telegraph to the Chief Constable of Birmingham asking urgently for more constables to be sent.

Possibly the head of the Birmingham police guessed that some of his own pet criminals were the cause of the appeal. He had had previous experience of how quickly a race paddock could become like a battle ground, so he sent off by the next train a contingent of officers. Today they could have been at Shrewsbury by car in a very short time but as it was they arrived too late to prevent a melée.

Just after the last race a rush was made from the course into the enclosure, headed by well-known Birmingham thieves, reinforced by some friends from London. The gate keepers were overpowered and Tattersall's ring invaded. Blows were freely exchanged and Ham was laid unconscious. For a moment or two there was something like panic amongst the bookmakers, for most of them had large sums of money in their cases. But then the gentlemen came to the rescue, and the ruffians were at last beaten. Lord Marcus Beresford was foremost in the defence and left his mark on several of them. He and his friends backed the small force of local constabulary and the attackers were surprised, defeated and some arrested. There was every probability that the trouble might have been renewed the following day but at breakfast the following morning thirty stalwart constables paraded in front of the Town Hall and this show of force had a deterrent effect.

There was no doubt that the leadership of Lord Marcus Beresford and his friends was responsible for the riot being quelled and for the ring-leaders being taken into custody. This crippled the Birmingham gang for a time but by no means put an end to the operations of those who escaped. They carried on till their companions were released and then there was a reunion and greater lawlessness than ever. For instance at Lincoln races on another occasion they drew out the wooden parade ring posts and threatened the bookmakers. Had not about fifty gentlemen and fox-hunting farmers followed the example of Lord Marcus and taken the field against them they would have won. Many of the gang would remember to the day of their death the thrashing they got on Lincoln racecourse. No mercy was shown to the villains, some were frightfully beaten, others had the clothes torn from their backs, and their ill gotten gains divided amongst their conquerors. Others took to the river to avoid greater evil. Despite the reputation of the Birmingham Boys for revenge, they never displayed any ill will to Lord Marcus Beresford. He used to tell amusing stories of meeting some of these desperadoes later. Once at Worcester he said a man seized his portmanteau to carry it from a cab to his train and when he offered him a shilling, the man replied: "I don't want your blasted bob, Marky, you gave me that at Shrewsbury," pointing to a scar on his face.

The Birmingham Boys became a real menace to many race meetings and threatened the very existence of a few of the smaller fixtures which they regularly raided. Indeed, it was partly owing to their attentions that the various racecourses started in the vicinity of Birmingham did not prosper.

The Four Oaks Park meeting near Birmingham was opened in 1881 being sponsored, planned, and managed by John Sheldon, who was so intimately associated with the Turf generally and around Birmingham in particular. In 1881 Sheldon set out with the determination that he would police the meeting so strictly that the gang of Birmingham roughs would have no quarter. Never before had there been so many police seen at a country race meeting. He realised that a bad beginning would damn the new fixture at the outset. There were rumours that the Birmingham race gang were to pay Four Oaks Park particular attention so the bank sent two of its officials in a cab with a policeman by the side of the driver and two inside, to collect the day's takings. A number of men well-known in the boxing ring were specially engaged and paid to keep an eye on the paddock ring, and stand-by to be handy in case of anything in the nature of a disturbance or attack being launched. These men knew all the old hands in the Birmingham gang. It is said that it cost more to police and guard those who patronised Four Oaks Park than it did to pay the whole of the expenses at some small country race meetings.

So far as organised attacks, and anything in the nature of a miniature riot — such as the Birmingham race gang had created at many little Turf fixtures — Four Oaks Park was immune. The Birmingham Boys saw that the staff work had been too good for their usual methods of bribery and collective terrorism, but their pick-pocketing activities were outrageous and this frightened away the expected crowds.

The majority of the Birmingham gang were men of a

vicious, broken-nosed, cauliflowered eared type. There were, however, exceptions. One of the leaders was Tom Jenison a tall, good looking man, who always dressed well, spoke with a cultured voice and would pass anywhere as a gentleman. To most regular racing men he was a mystery. He was known by sight to all of them, was invariably alone, stayed at the best hotels, played a good game of billiards and cards and paid up when he lost. Jenison always stood his corner never asked for information about horses, appeared to have plenty of money, didn't bet much and left many guessing as to his business. He was responsible for some of the hotel robberies when men, who had collected considerable sums from the ring, had had their wallets removed from their rooms during the night when asleep after drinking too much champagne — Jenison ensuring that the wine flowed.

He was at Four Oaks Park on the opening day, maybe making notes for future operations on the part of his more cut throat subordinates. They had made Sutton Coldfield races a den of iniquity and a place at which the regular racing fraternity kept their pockets very tightly buttoned. Sheldon was the presiding genius at this meeting too and admitted that "the villains from Birmingham", as he called them, had defeated him there. That was why at the very outset he took such precautionary measures with the new fixture at Four Oaks Park. Even so, the unfortunate meeting had the seeds of failure in it from the start. For one thing, some of the Stewards were quite impossible, and could only have been exalted into that position on account of the money they had put into the course. One Steward at least would have been unfitted for the post of shop-walker in a third rate millinery establishment. He knew nothing about racing, and it was depressing to find no one in the palatial stand but half-a-dozen or so fishmongers, covered all over with gigantic diamonds as if with scales. Anyway the meetings that were held ran at a hefty loss, and soon Four Oaks Park was abandoned.

Another Birmingham fixture doomed by the gang was Hall

Green. This meeting, too, became a hot-bed of dangerous roughs, despite all the efforts of James Page, the clerk of the course. I raced there up to 1910 but this fixture, too, was doomed. As the more recent death of Birmingham's final course indicated, the people of the City have always been more keen on football than horse-racing. The different courses might have stood a chance but for the gangland reign of terror, but disinterest coupled with fear meant that they never had a fair chance.

One way and another the Birmingham Boys killed the meetings at Sutton Coldfield, Four Oaks Park and Hall Green.

Another fixture spoilt by the gangs was the attractive seaside meeting at Scarborough. Tom Devereux, who was Fred Archer's commissioner when jockeys betted openly, told me: "I think for rowdyism, welshers and general uncontrolled villainy, the old Scarborough racecourse was the worst I was ever on — and I have been on most in Britain. I remember in 1893 a whole trainload of 300 known crooks, 'boys', welshers and violent blackmailers being collected before racing started. They were marched to the station and sent off by train — a sight never before or since witnessed in connection with the Turf. I have seen Scarborough racegoers laid out with stakes and bottles the length of the Grandstand enclosure. The number of police in those days was absolutely no check. The gangs used to raid these country meetings, knowing that there was very little to prevent them having all their own way. Also that they would come across a lot of country fellows, who probably never went racing more than the few days a year on their local course. I remember seeing two pick-pockets covering each other as they went through the yokels. I pointed them out to a policeman, and one was arrested. As I was coming out of the subsequent York meeting, a gang surrounded me and said: 'You're the bastard who gave our pals away at Scarborough.' One of them produced a knife and I was sure that I was in for it. I had a good deal of money on me, and feared the worst. Just in time a group of my pals arrived on the scene and 'the boys' vanished."

Miles I'Anson told me that Scarborough gave him more anxiety than any other of the many meetings he controlled, when he was clerk of the course there. The fixture had an imposing grandstand, and there had been racing at the town since 1751. Nevertheless Flat racing was killed by the gangsters in 1893. National Hunt sport continued until 1907, though, and I was at the final meeting.

There is no doubt that racecourse policemen were bribed, "not to see" what was going on. This is what an ex-detective told me in 1950:

"When I first joined the force I was detailed for racecourse work at Doncaster during the St Leger week. As a rule the same detectives were engaged because they were supposed to know all the Birmingham gang and the 'Boys' from London, Leeds and elsewhere. A senior inspector told another officer he had better take me round. This was done and I was sounded, 'We always make a bit for ourselves here, you know' I was told. 'Well, I'm a stranger' I replied 'and am here to do as I'm told.' I was taken back to the inspector to whom it was reported 'everything will be all right.' At the end of the four days racing I was handed £50 as my share of the proceeds which could not have been anything but the bribes of those who paid for non-interference, for the £50 was apart altogether from my pay. If I, a young constable, received such a sum how much did others in higher rank get to shut their eyes to the doings of the gang? I believe one racecourse detective died worth £22,000."

Newcastle, in common with Glasgow, Leeds, Mexborough and Birmingham had its race gang, which for long was very active on courses and race trains in the North country. They numbered in their ranks not only clever and well-known criminals but desperate men who would stop at nothing to secure money, or to satisfy the revenge which they always promised if they were given away.

Perhaps the "Newcastle Boys" were best organised, most feared and made their biggest hauls when under the leadership of Donald Mark. He lived in Gateshead and had, I fancy, originally been in an office. Anyhow, he was not only a man of some education, but of commanding and gentlemanly appearance. Well-dressed, tall, with a certain presence, there was nothing of the Bill Sykes about him. He had no scars on his face to tell of conflicts or to at once arouse the suspicions of those who did not know him and his confederates by sight. The police did, so did many regular race-goers and probably all the bookmakers who stood up on the Northern circuit. Donald was very friendly with the notorious Birmingham gang and was one of their allies in the memorable razor and stiletto fight with the Sabini gang on the Epsom-London road during Derby week. Donald — daring, strong, fearless, often really impudent in the tricks he played — at last met an enemy stronger than the bookmakers' ex-bruisers, stronger than the police, stronger than his own indomitable will. He was attacked by consumption and died in Walkergate Hospital, Newcastle. His name will live for long in the underworld of Tyneside, and amongst those Turfites of all classes who knew — and maybe feared — the Newcastle Boys.

In 1917 Donald was chosen as leader of the Newcastle Boys to succeed Big Stumps. The latter was arrested for receiving jewellery stolen from a shop in the Cloth Market, and was sent for trial at the Assizes. He got 15 months, and at the trial Donald with a lot more of the Boys were in court. They heard Big Stumps confess that he had on several occasions assisted the police and Donald was at once chosen to be leader. A favourite meeting place of the gang was in Nelson Street and at Grey's Monument. They had their own code of signals, as clever and as well understood as those of the tick-tack men on the course, the only difference being that whereas the tick-tack signs mean one thing today and another tomorrow, those employed by the Boys never varied. They at once conveyed to the other members that they were being watched, that the signaller "had someone in tow", that assistance was wanted, that some individual who was being followed had already been "gone through" and was "no bon" or that someone else indicated was worth attention.

The Newcastle Boys had many good points, at any rate as compared with the even more notorious, more violent and often really inhuman gangs from Birmingham and Glasgow. They had to defend themselves on occasions both from capture or from a mauling. Well, self-preservation is the first law of nature to the animal, the law-abiding citizen, and also the crook. As I remember, the last gang which made Newcastle its headquarters and travelled the northern race meetings were a witty, amusing crowd, who gave us many a hearty laugh at their criticism of railway officials when race specials were late or over-crowded. Their voices could be heard from one end of a crowded station platform to the other, and they got a seat whoever else had to stand — although their wild rushes to enter carriages were often part of their pocket-picking exploits.

Who does not remember "Luggy" an ex-boxer, and associated with the Newcastle gang, lashing porters and others with his tongue and telling them he was only travelling "by the rattler" (train) because he had given both his chauffeurs a holiday. When Luggy was making a little crowd of "mugs" roar with laughter by his sallies and well-assumed indignation he was skilfully going through their pockets. The lighthearted chatter was Luggy's carefully rehearsed cover — while the "pigeons" listened and laughed they overlooked his hands. This was a case of the slickness of the voice deceiving the eye.

Another name which involuntarily crops up when discussing the Tyneside race gang of our time is that of James Carter who was eventually executed for the murder of a sailor. Apart altogether from this crime, and others which the archives of the Newcastle police could doubtless disclose, had he put down on paper the hauls he made on race courses between Ripon and Stockton, Newcastle and Carlisle, his memoirs would have been astounding. Some of the gangsters made it a rule not to take toll from the regulars. They went for the "mugs" who flashed their winnings, who paraded their money, and almost asked to be relieved of it. Jimmy Carter had no code of honour. He would blackmail a bookie, and let him know quite plainly that if he didn't part he would not be allowed to stand-up and bet. He would follow a trainer whom he had seen collect from the ring and go on following him till he had got hold of that money. He was a violent fellow, not averse to knocking anyone on the head with a bottle. Carter would try to push a man out of a train corridor on to the line if he owed a grudge, or had reason to believe they had "peached" upon any of the gang. Among those who worked with him were "Drummer" and "The Rabbit". There was an ex-jockey, too, who on being refused a licence, took to tipping, pocket-tapping and eventually became a fully accepted member of the Newcastle Gang.

I recall a real thrill I got when staying a night in Newcastsle for Hexham Races in 1909. A party of us went to the theatre run by Dick Thornton, who was then closely associated with Tommy Courtenay and others in running Blaydon and Boldon flapping meetings. His theatre was naturally the one to which sportsmen gravitated, and to which — with perfectly peaceable interest — some of the leaders of the Newcastle Race Gang also went to spend their evenings. In the interval I was introduced to a big, powerful, square-shouldered, fair haired man in the bar — a clever talker and most amusing. He knew all the trainers I was with and was known, at any rate by sight, by them. He lacked nothing in self-confidence, insisted on paying for drinks, made us laugh and talked knowingly regarding the morrow's programme. When he had gone I asked who he was and was told "He is one of the heads of the Newcastle Boys — not a bad fellow! He'll do anything to help the regulars who go racing, and it's well to keep in with him." In the folly of my youth I felt that I had been basking in the sunshine of distinguished company. I often saw this character afterwards, more particularly when travelling to northern race meetings than in the paddock. He was eventually arrested for a razor attack on a bookmaker.

Another gang leader, Wally Brock, saw that if he owned a racehorse or two that it would give him considerable status, and added opportunity to catch those who are always seeking information. He was a good judge of a horse and of form, and when the promising winner of a selling plate was knocked down to him, a very respectable trainer at once buttoned him at the sale ring and asked if he might be allowed to train the animal. The gangster soon bought one or two more horses which went into the same stable without the trainer having the least suspicion that his new patron was one of "The Boys" and that the animals he trained were merely to be used as sprats to catch mackerels. The trainer's fees were regularly paid, he found the owner a knowledgeable man who made his own entries and decided in which events his platers would run. So well did he select the course best suited to them, and the events in which they had least opposition that he won many races, and profited by backing his runners.

But what he won from the ring was of less account than the entrée that owning winning horses gave him into certain circles. Now here is the trainer's story of one way in which the charmed title of "owner" served his gang:

"I found out the racket when things got so hot they had to clear off to France. The racehorses were nothing more or less than decoys to attract pigeons. The cleverest part of the whole business was that none of the gang, and I knew many of them by sight, ever went near or seemed to know my patron — their leader as I found he was — in the paddock. If I had seen any signs of intimacy between them I might have been suspicious. The only hint I got was from one or two professional backers, who made some such remarks as 'A nice sort of bloke you're training for now!' I put this down as the result of some personal grievance or jealousy. As I got paid regularly and understood my man was something in the City, I asked no questions. Later, as I've said, the whole ramp came out, and I found I'd had horses in my stable owned by one of the biggest crooks in creation. I believe he had been to a public school, and had moved in good society. He seemed to me a gentleman, never pestered me about other patron's horses and didn't bother me with visits like some of my owners who were never out of the yard. His wife seemed quite up to his stamp, and I afterwards found out that she and a girl who was always with her assisted in bringing in the lambs to be shorn. They would arrive at the railway station early on race days, and would walk up and down the race special until they discovered someone whom they had marked down beforehand, or knew to have more money than experience of the world. My patron would enter the carriage in which the intended victim was seated, and later the ladies would join him. The leader would be hailed as a pal into whose company they had come by accident but with evident pleasure. 'Now we shall get to know something worth backing' one of the last arrivals would remark. After some general conversation the owner would say in a semi-confidential whisper, 'Mine must have a chance, but I'll be able to tell you for certain when we get there and I hear the strength of things from my trainer and what the jockeys say in the weighing-room.' If the supposed 'mug' pricked his ears or appeared interested — as so many men are when they hear someone speak who had the entrée to the weighing-room — a whispered conversation with him quickly followed. They arranged to meet him in the paddock, where they would kindly let his commission 'go with theirs'. That day, of course, the 'good thing' did not win. The ruse generally worked and should it fail when the victim was hustled either as he stepped out of the train or on his way to the paddock gates. He would certainly lose his wallet if he were followed with this intention, and so rapidly would it be handed to one of the others and on to one of the women confederates that arrest or recovery was impossible.

"One horse the leader of this gang owned had been passed on to him as part payment of a debt incurred at cards. The animal could go a bit, and once or twice when it won, young men who had recently come into money had been told by the gangster chief to back it. They did so, were highly delighted with their luck and their new-found friend, had several bottles of champagne on the course to celebrate, formed a party for dinner in town, and afterwards accompanied their host and his very jolly and entertaining friends to his private residence. There was more wine and cards, and then came the test of skill and finesse — the correct judgement of the character of the youths with whom they were dealing. Should they be allowed to win at cards that night with a view to a bigger haul in the future or should they have all the ready they had in their possession taken from them forthwith? Often the wealthy pigeons were given some more corn and a waiting game was successfully played. One young officer fell into their hands. He was a first-class shot, and they persuaded him to go over to Monte Carlo with them to win a fortune. Impressed by the astuteness of the leader of the gang, the officer handed him £10,000 to be invested at the best possible odds available on his gun against the birds. The gang saw to it that his cartridges were faked, kept his stake in their pockets and bled him white.

"The end came when they got in tow a very rich but hard-headed manufacturer from the North of England. He was too cautious, and the most they could get out of him at their swell house was about £50 a time. It was decided to try another plan before letting him off the hook. Getting him to their headquarters one night they doped him and put him to bed. Towards morning when he had partially slept off the effects of the dope, one of the women crept naked into his bed, and my patron followed with a camera in his hand. The rich manufacturer was married and when awakened by his apparently infuriated host he saw there was nothing for it but to square him with £1,000 and clear out. But he let Scotland Yard know the whole of the circumstances. They kept the house under observation, but before they could get hold of the principal he skipped across the channel. Two of his right-hand-men, however, were arrested and got five years each. What became of the women remains a mystery. I never saw them on a racecourse again, and the remainder of the gang operated singly. Minus their leader, they flew at much smaller game or went out of the racecourse business entirely."

CHAPTER SEVEN

OUR BETTERS

I remember once suggesting to Sir Loftus Bates that he should place on record some of his Turf memories. His reply was: "If I put all I knew into print, half of those on the Turf stage would be warned off." Sir Loftus and I started our Turf careers about the same time. In the early days Stewards were often chosen because of rank, social position, or the fact that they gave a lot of entries to the meetings at which they acted officially. Many of them were mere figureheads, who knew little about the rules of racing. They had not sufficient knowledge of the wiles of jockeys and trainers to enable them to "read" a race correctly, and to note incidents quite obvious to those able to recognise that some horses were not very "busy". They were not quick enough to note that other horses were running to try and hoodwink the handicapper. Sir Loftus used to tell the story of George Maclachlan, chairman of the old Hamilton Park Race Company — and so a Steward at the meeting. He did not approve of objections because entries were difficult to get for Scottish meetings and he reckoned that executives could not afford to offend any owner or trainer.

Once, when the second horse could obviously have won had he been "wanted", Sir Loftus said: "I suppose you will interview the rider?" To this Maclachlan replied: "It was what I would call a very vulgar finish, but it is no use doing anything that will cause bad blood." This same easy going Steward won five consecutive races at Hamilton Park on July 19, 1902. He was keen to create a record by winning the sixth in which he owned the favourite. There were three runners, and one of them was known to be a non-tryer . . . . or so Maclachlan was led to believe. Anyway, he discounted this horse and bought the other at an inflated price. With the first and second favourites both carrying his colours, he climbed the stands full of confidence that the six-timer would be achieved. Unfortunately for this canny Scot, the "dead meat" came very much alive and won easily to net a sizeable coup for its connections.

What some describe as "the good old days of racing" were so in some respects. They were more friendly, more leisurely, less commercialised, easier-going, with a more open-air-sporting-club aspect. On the other hand there is no denying the fact that there was far more villainy, more "arranged" races, and more cases of substitution of one horse for another — particularly old horses for young ones.

Indeed, I am convinced that half the stories of Turf malpractices one hears today are mere paddock froth, blown into sensations by irresponsible scaremongers. There is much closer vigilance today, more watchful officials and Stewards who know every move on the board from A to Z. There are exceptions, of course, but trainers, jockeys — and owners — who try to be "wide" all eventually learn that the straight and narrow is the only way to lasting Turf success.

I have lived long enough on the Turf to see three or four generations of jockeys come and go; and at least two generations of owners, trainers, officials and professional backers succeed one another. I have known most paddock personalities intimately, have had almost weekly contact with them, have "felt their pulse", and have been in the close confidence of many. I can emphatically say that the indictment I heard the late Sir Abe Bailey make when he was chief guest at the Gimcrack Club dinner, is far less applicable today.

Sir Abe stated: "It is said that all those who go racing are rogues and vagabonds. That may not be true. But it IS true that all the rogues and vagabonds go racing." Lady Ashburton once said: "If I were to begin my life again, I would go to the Turf for friends. They seem to me to be the only people who really hold close together. It may be that each knows something that might hang the other — but the effect is altogether delightful."

During my lifetime on the Turf I have met fascinating men. Some of them were little known, others internationally famous. All played their different roles in racing lore, and several made lasting impressions on me. Certainly there were far more outstanding chracters on the Turf years ago than there are today. Two of the best known North country regulars at the turn of the century were Tommy Courtney of Sunderland, and Billy Leng of Copmanthorpe, near York. Both of them were seen at every North country meeting, and both exported a lot of horses to the Continent. They had a market for any animal which had been placed in a race in England, and Tommy Courtney was the main supplier of runners for the Belgium Turf.

Tommy sometimes kept some of them in Britain to try to pick up a seller before shipping them abroad and he was also involved with the "flapping" meetings at Boldon and Blaydon. Tommy got me to attend one or two Blaydon meetings and I found it was a case of, "I'll win today and let you win tomorrow." How the bookmakers got their cards marked defeats me, yet it was possible to back a horse at Blaydon to win several hundreds.

Eventually there was a riot on the course and the crowd wrecked the stands and weighing room. Blaydon died unhonoured in 1915 — but not unsung because the song "Blaydon Races" is to Northumberland what "John Peel" is to Cumberland. It is because of the song not the races that Tyneside spent thousands of pounds in 1961 commemorating the centenary of the first Blaydon racemeeting. Those who remember the fixture think it would be better forgotten.

I have known many "easy come — easy go" personalities and have had tremendous fun and enjoyment in their company. Bob Sievier was probably the most incredible of this happy band, while Bob Robson was undoubtedly the kindest and most gentle hearted and Sir Abe Bailey the richest. At the same time I have always been very impressed with the dedication of the true professionals like Charlie Hannam, and especially, Alex Bird.

Most trainers bet. This has always been true. John Porter told me that he received in fees only just sufficient to live on — but he became rich by saddling 1,063 winners. "If I had been a betting man I might have been a millionaire but I rarely had a bet," he told me. In those days top trainers received between £2.50 and £3 a week for each horse in their charge, while some of the provincial trainers charged only £1.50. When Matt Dawson trained for the millionaire Scottish owner James Merry his salary was only £250 a year.

William I'Anson was a very heavy gambler. He trained for the Northern Confederacy a group who bet on a lavish scale. His father, who had a large stable at Gullane in Scotland before moving to Highfield at Malton advised: "William, if you take my tip you will not bet . . . . But if you do bet — BET!" William certainly did. I have known him have £1,000 on one of his horses when I had £1.

William I'Anson Snr., saddled the last Northern trained Epsom Derby victor, Blair Athol who won in 1864. Bred and trained by I'Anson this colt made Turf history by winning the Derby on his first appearance in public. Blair Athol started at 14-1 and the trainer won £15,000 from his wager. Three stable patrons shared £64,000 between them. Another sizeable gamble was landed when the colt won the St. Leger.

Young William started training in 1869 and won 1,300 races before he retired in 1912. He won the 1880 Oaks with Jenny Howlett — a filly that underlined the unreliability of home trials. Jenny Howlett cost only 1,300 guineas and both she and her stable companion Bonnie Marden won races as two-year-olds. They did so well during the winter that I'Anson felt certain they had the Oaks between them. A few days before the race they were galloped together at Highfield and Bonnie

Marden stayed best and won impressively. She was backed accordingly but Jenny Howlett, the 33-1 chance, won the Epsom classic in a canter with Bonnie Marden second.

William I'Anson and Bob Robson were great friends. Bob born in 1853 won his first race as an amateur jockey on Spider at Wetherby in 1883. In 1894 he bought the Branton Court Estate, Farnham, near Knaresborough and began to train Compton Vyner's steeplechasers and hurdlers. Throughout his career he never had a horse in the stable that cost more than £300 — "but nearly all that I did train were good, honest animals, and I really loved them as pals," he once told me. Bob had a wonderful way with horses, and the knack of getting the very best out of them. He won 30 races with Chapeltown a cheap reject from a Newmarket Yard. "Lewis cost me a tenner and was supposed to be a mad horse when I got him. I won several races with him, he went kindly for me and we were always the best of friends. I once took Lewis to Haydock and was dressing to ride him myself when Abington Baird pressed me to accept £25 for the mount. He was keen to ride winners no matter in what sort of Flat races so I told him that Lewis could not beat Baneret and in any case I wanted to be second. He still persisted in wanting to ride Lewis so I gave way. It was a good race and Baird was only beaten a neck. I got £600 to £400 Baneret and got £125 for Lewis finishing second — but Baird forgot about the £25."

Bob had the wealthy Yorkshire owner Herbert Rhodes annoyed with him for entering his good horse Count Oso in a little £40 race at the, now defunct, Brocklesby meeting in 1909. Bob, however, reasoned thus: "Never mind the stake, you like to back your horses when they win. Count Oso can't be beaten at Brocklesby and will start at nice odds. You get a dozen of your friends to lend you their nom de plumes with their starting price offices, and I'll get a few of my pals to do the same. On the way to Brocklesby we'll send wires from village post offices backing Count Oso for a pony with each of the starting price men. There is no post office or blower on

Brocklesby course and telegrams have to be brought by bicycle from the nearest post office two or three miles away, so there will be no chance of any money getting back to the ring there." Many of poor Bob's hoped for betting coups went awry, and his financial status was very precarious but this one came off brilliantly. Count Oso won easily at odds of 4-1 and the winnings amounted to over £3,000.

The Hon. George Lambton in his young days, often risked a good deal of money in Turf plunges. He had a useful, old horse called Durham, trained by Tom Green at Hambleton. Thinking he might get a better price in a little Northern race if he put up Mr. Holmes, he gave him the mount and asked Lord Lurgan to get him £1,000 on. This Lord Lurgan did, he and his friends also helping themselves. At the last moment the well-known Scottish sportsman Johnny Martin, asked Lambton if he would ride a horse of his in the race. Lambton told him he had a runner he thought certain to win but Martin persuaded him to ride his animal. The result was that Lambton found himself going much better than Holmes on Durham, and eventually won the race to the disgust of his friends — and his own loss.

Except when I really fancied one of the racehorses I owned in those pre-1914 days, I seldom wagered. When I was a judge, of course, I was not allowed to bet. As for "straight from the horses mouth" information, I have had any amount of that — often several owners and trainers telling me that their particular horse was a "guaranteed certainty" for the same race on the card. I have seen lots of men, students of form, astute and methodical gamblers, try to break — or shake — the ring. These professional gamblers give their whole thought, time and energy to selecting and backing winners. The only man to succeed since the war is my friend Alex Bird. The others have gambled in thousands for a time, but eventually they have disappeared from the Turf. Some to stay home and count their losses without disgrace, others barred from entering racecourses because they cannot settle their betting debts. Others had fun and could smile at misfortune. In 1931 Herbert Fitzroy Clayton got £100,000 to

£100 that he did not win the Cesarewitch and Cambridgeshire. The wager nearly came off too, for Clayton's Disarmament won the Cambridgeshire and his Six Wheeler — both trained by Capt. Elsey at Malton — was second in the Cesarewitch. Neither the loss of £100, or the near miss of winning £100,000 mattered two hoots to Clayton.

In recent times we had the bluff, genial Edmund Brown of Doncaster with the big string of horses — in four of five stables — and a lot of brood mares at Stapleton Park, a place rich in Turf history. He bet like smoke and I always found him a most cheery, rough diamond. We had a standing joke that I was promoted or demoted in rank according to what I handed him in the way of club badges, luncheon and tea-tickets. On occasions when he had a lot of runners and he was treated more generously than my instructions really allowed, I was a general. Sometimes I was reduced to lance-corporal. Once he complained to Tom Petch at Redcar that although he had five or six runners and a lot more entries, I had given him only two luncheon tickets and complimentary badges, Mr. Petch, always ripe for a bit of fun and practical joke, said "Give them to me, I'll see that you're properly treated." He set off as if for my office and a few minutes later returned to Edmund without ever seeing me, and handing him one luncheon ticket, said "He says you're only entitled to one!"

I knew and liked the strange Bob Sievier — who published the *Winning Post* for which I worked and by which I was attacked. Lady Luck played every possible prank on Robert Standish Sievier. The fortunes of this astonishing man wavered like an aspen leaf in a gale. He gambled very heavily with mixed success; trained his mighty filly Sceptre to win four classic races; was "warned off"; had many millions of pounds through his hands, but went bankrupt five times and died penniless. On one of his many appearances in court he was described as "a gambler pure and simple" which prompted the immediate retort: "Pure I may be — but I am not simple." Born in 1860, Sievier's start to life set the pattern for its span. Reputedly expelled from Sherborne for making a book that effectively deprived his classmates of their pocket money, he started his working life as an actor in company with Jimmy Glover. Later he wrote plays that no one would produce, but clearly his grounding in the art of stage craft was never to be forgotten throughout his stranger than fiction life.

Failure as a dramatist perhaps prompted Sievier to go to Australia, and there he used his schoolday bookmaking experience to teach racegoers a lesson. Apparently Australian layers were then insisting that clients must find the winners of two races at a time in order to bet. Sievier, making a book under the name "Bob Sutton" offered odds in the English style and earned immediate popularity.

Dick Luckman, for many years the *Daily Express* racing correspondent, mentions in his autobiography: "I first saw Robert Sievier making a book on 'The Hill' at Flemington. The Hill is a natural mound from which one can throw a pebble onto the roof of the grandstand, and just as good a view of racing can be obtained as in the enclosure itself. A newcomer is always noted and discussed. "Robert Sutton" was very well dressed in new light English tweeds which were our envy. I can see him now calling the odds fearlessly, and taking in a bunch of ready money . . . . In the ring at Randwick, Sydney, after the third race of the big day he told punters that he had no money with him. They could bet with him if they liked, but not for ready money. Such audacity! And they rolled up some giving the ready, but to each one he was emphatic that there would be no settlement until the following afternoon. I think that he won six of seven hundred pounds over the three races which remained on the card. His open talk about being short of money appealed to many, especially as he laid good odds."

When Sievier returned to England he evidently had a substantial bank balance, and at once set about making it even bigger. In Australia a horse called The Grafter had impressed so much that Sievier backed it to win him £35,000 in the City and Suburban. He rightly judged that The Grafter would be ideally suited to Epsom's ups and downs and difficult corners.

In the same year he won £30,000 over Diamond Jubilee's Derby, and was £53,000 to the good at the end of Epsom week. "It was always my practice to play up my winnings" he recorded later, noting that he had won £250,000 in one especially lucky run.

Soon Sievier was established on an estate in Bedfordshire where he entertained W. G. Grace, William Yardley and other famous players during cricket weeks. A lavish entertainer, only the very best was good enough for his guests. Once when dining at Romano's he took a fancy to the wine that was served. Calling for Romano he said: "This is good wine. Have you much of it." When "The Roman" replied that he had, Sievier ordered: "Send me fifty dozen." Evidently, though, the wine was so enjoyable that it did not last long — with the help of a few friends Sievier finished it all in three weeks.

In 1900 he paid 10,000 guineas for a colt which he named Toddington after his estate. His trainer, Charles Morton, was sceptical about this extremely high price. The first engagement for the youngster was the Woodcote Stakes at Epsom, but beforehand Morton staged a trial at even weights with Sievier's plater, Crarae. After Crarae had won the owner commented: "You have asked the colt to do too much," but Morton replied: "Not me, the trouble is that you have given far too much for Toddington. However that will not stop him winning the Woodcote." Indeed at Epsom Siever successfully invested £5,000 on Crarae in a selling race, and twice as much on his two-year-old. These winnings were the nucleus of his huge gamble on Diamond Jubilee the following day. Then at Kempton Park the following Saturday both Crarae and Toddington won again with the owner playing up his winnings. Toddington won a £1,000 race, but split a pastern so it was his last public appearance.

Morton, who saddled 11 classic winners, trained for Sievier until tempted to leave by Jack Barnato Joel the father of Jim Joel and a Rand Millionaire. Morton described Sievier as "one of the world's greatest ever plungers." Morton was responsible for the two-year-old preparation of the peerless Sceptre, saddling her to win the Woodcote Stakes (£925), the July Stakes (£1,530) and to finish third in the Champagne Stakes. Bred by the Duke of Westminster in 1899, Sievier gave 10,000 guineas for Sceptre, and himself trained the filly as a three-year-old when she won the Two Thousand Guineas, the One Thousand Guineas, the Oaks, the St James Palace Stakes, and the St Leger. She was also beaten a head in the Lincolnshire Handicap, ran fourth in the Derby, second in the Sussex Stakes and the Park Hill Stakes, fifth in the Coronation Stakes and unplaced in the Grand Prix de Paris.

Sievier lost £30,000 when Sceptre was beaten a head in the Lincolnshire Handicap. Ridden by Herbert Randall, son of a Northampton boot manufacturer, the filly won the Two Thousand Guineas in a canter in record time. On the following Friday she won the One Thousand although handicapped by a twisted plate which had to be wrenched off at the last moment. The owner-trainer backed her to win £33,000 over the Derby, but ten days before the race found her lame. Sievier patched her up and sent her to Epsom supremely confident, but she finished fourth.

At this there were ugly rumours that the owner had won a fortune laying against her. To make matters worse, Sceptre was pulled out again on the Friday and won the Oaks in a canter at 5-2. There was no truth in the rumours though. Far from it, in fact, because Sievier had to persuade Messrs. Pratts, the Epsom stake holders, to advance him Sceptre's Oaks winnings so that he could pay his Derby losses to bookmakers at the Victoria Club and so avoid being black-listed on the following Monday. Sievier dismissed his jockey after Sceptre was beaten in the Coronation Cup, and the next day she won the St James' Palace Stakes. At Goodwood she was beaten in her first race at the meeting, but two days later won the Nassau Stakes. Before the St Leger Sievier rigged a trial with Sceptre against Horatio Bottomley's Wargrave. This prompted Sceptre to drift in the Doncaster market to 6-1, while Bottomley was so impressed by the trial win of his Ebor Victor Wargrave that he laid Sievier £5,000 to £1,000 that the filly would not win the St. Leger. All were taken in, and Bottomley in particular paid his losses in very bad grace. During her four year old career, Sceptre won the Hardwicke Stakes, the Jockey Club Stakes, Duke of York Stakes, and finished second in the Eclipse Stakes. In all she won 13 of her 25 races worth £38,225. She was also second five times and third on three occasions.

The Bloodstock Review (Vol XV) notes: "It is always hazardous to compare racing giants of our own day with those of former periods, but it is hardly conceivable that there was ever a greater racing mare than Sceptre." The writer continues: "I am justified in describing Bob Sievier as the most picturesque figure we have seen on the Turf for the last 30 years. His career has been one of wildly fluctuating fortune. Within the space of a few months he would be poor, rich and then poor again — but whatever the state of his finances he was invariably optimistic and nonchalant . . . . "

That nonchalance must have been shaken, however, at the end of 1902. For, despite Sceptre's many triumphs, Sievier had to borrow money to pay his debts. Eventually, too, he was forced to sell the filly for 25,000 guineas after she had failed to reach her reserve at public auction. Morton, who had tremendous admiration for his onetime patron, always insisted that Sceptre would have won all five classics had she not been misguidedly prepared for the Lincolnshire Handicap tilt. The trainer had many wonderful stories about Sievier. "I first made his acquaintance in the early nineties not long after he had returned from Australia" writes Morton in his autobiography, "and I soon came to know well the man who charmed everybody he met by his bonhomie and fascinating personality."

The trainer adds: "Without a doubt Bob has been one of the pluckiest — as well as the luckiest — plungers ever known. On one particular occasion I remember well, he intended running some horses at Doncaster and had invited a house party for the occasion. Coming back with the horses from exercise I went into his bedroom to tell him the news, and he showed me a letter which he had accidentally opened. It was addressed to a well-known bookmaker, and how it had happened among Bob's letters nobody ever discovered. It contained important news for a racing man. Written by a stable lad in the employ of W. G. Stevens of Compton, it disclosed that a horse called King's Lynn would win the Scarborough Stakes. The boy wanted the modest sum of £2 for his intelligence. The favourite for the race was Santoi, a celebrated stayer. The Ring asked for 2 to 5 on Santoi and Bob, after having a look at King's Lynn, proceeded to have a few hundred on the outsider. And what must he do but go up to the bookmaker to whom the letter had been addressed and ask him what price he would lay about King's Lynn. I think Bob took 100-7 to quite a lot of money and, as is only fitting, King's Lynn won in a canter."

Morton must have been reluctant to see Sceptre leave his stable, but notes: "I had received a lucrative offer from J. B. Joel to take over his horses and Bob, for the time being, became his own trainer." Of Sceptre's Lincolnshire Handicap defeat the trainer writes: "Generally speaking I do not approve of running three-year-olds, especially fillies, in a hard race like the Lincoln. Sceptre is probably the greatest filly the English Turf has ever known and even she went under, though only by a head. It is an unfair handicap to ask a three-year-old, who may be only a young one at that, to run in a gruelling race against older horses in such an event, which is invariably run at a tremendous pace from start to finish. Such a severe task might very well spoil a good three year old for the remainder of its racing career, apart from the difficulty, if you really have the Classics in mind, of keeping horses in training before the Derby and Oaks come on."

Always fashionably dressed, the well-made figure of Sievier was imposing, and short lived though it was, his stage career had taught him how to make the most of his presence. His walrus moustache shielded a splendid smile, which must have flashed at its brightest when he made that famous "pure not simple" court interjection. Doubtless the thespian Sievier had many happy moments in the dock — but his frequent court appearances cost him dear in both money and repute. In 1904 he sued the well known amateur jockey Sir James Duke, who had accused him of card sharping. Not only did he lose in the High Court, but was subjected to such a damaging cross-examination by the defence that he was "warned off" by the Jockey Club. The evidence that he gave about his Turf activities was one of the sensations of the era.

Not allowed on a racecourse, Sievier decided to again try his hand at writing — but not plays, this time. Instead he founded *The Winning Post* which he made a scurrilous sheet of racing gossip and information. Sievier used *The Winning Post* to attack anyone who incurred his displeasure — and so was never short of subject matter. The paper once even attacked me as already recorded and after a continued onslaught on him in the paper, Jack Barnato Joel sued Sievier alleging attempted blackmail.

There were several other legal actions before the Jockey Club removed their ban in 1910. Once back on the Turf Sievier was a happy man again. In 1912 he landed a £30,000 Cesarewitch coup with Warlingham, and bought Fitzroy House, Newmarket. Installed at Newmarket he set out to become the uncrowned king of the town, giving huge parties for his friends and presenting the local needy with ribs of beef and sacks of coal. Unfortunately many of the tradesmen never received their due. Again training his own horses he won the 1919 Lincolnshire Handicap with Royal Bucks, who went on to take the City and Suburban a few weeks later. But these achievements might not have been. Richard Wootton sued him for libel over an article in *The Winning Post*. Sievier fought the action and after a hearing lasting a week Wootton was awarded a farthing damages — and had his trainer's licence taken from him by the Jockey Club. A wealthy and revengeful man, Wootton decided to try and finish Sievier. In 1920 he engaged detectives to uncover the gambler's past, and flooded the streets and racecourses with a pamphlet containing a damning indictment. Sievier had either to sue for libel or be warned off again. Sir Partrick Hastings appeared for Wootton, and again Sievier was subjected to a lengthy, piercing and extremely damaging cross-examination. Nevertheless Sievier won his case — but only got his farthing back.

When Bob Sievier died he owed the ring "two fortunes". He had gambled recklessly, often investing £10,000 on a horse. His wife Lady Mabel Emily Louisa Brundenell-Bruce, elder sister of the fourth Marquis of Aylesbury, had left him after seeing her fortune disappear. Also he had been made bankrupt five times, during his hectic life packed with contradictions.

Sir Abe Bailey was yet another personality to brighten the Turf in my younger days. Born in 1864 he was an impulsive man who kept his trainers on the hop, gambled hugely — and sometimes sold his fleet of horses because they were not good enough. This livewire owner made a giant fortune in the South African gold rush — and dropped about £1,000,000 of his cash on the British Turf.

As an owner-breeder he was successful. Gambling, though, cost him dear. The failures far outnumbered the coups. Sir Abe was seldom prepared to accept that all his horses were not guaranteed world-beaters. He kept a large string and seldom had less than £5,000 on each of them when they ran. Only a vastly rich man could have carried on at that pace. Luckily for the British Turf — and the bookmakers — this South African was a Croesus. For his trainers — they included Harry Cottrill, Reg Day, Joe Lawson, Hon. George Lambton and Atty Persse — times cannot always have been rosy. Sir Abe was impatient with them, his jockeys and his horses. Often the remedy was a clear-out of his racers.

Sir Abe, powerfully built, ruddy complexioned and happy faced, was born in the Transvaal. He was associated with the Joels in the Johannesburg gold-rush, and made a fortune on the Rand. Coming to this country at the turn of the century he married the Hon. Mary, daughter of the fifth Lord Rossmore.

Sir Abe was one of His Majesty's Lieutenants for the City of London (1902-8) and a captain in the Sussex Imperial Yeomanry in 1915. He was elected to the Jockey Club in 1929. In his homeland he was a Member of Parliament, and he served throughout the South African War, winning six clasps to his King's and Queen's medals. Sir Abe enjoyed his life in England. He entertained lavishly at his home in London – throwing a particularly large party there before leaving it for the last time to return to South Africa in the Autumn of 1939. For three years he had been seriously ill, and phlebitis had meant the amputation of both legs. Nevertheless he refused to give in and had returned to England in 1939 to see some of his fancied horses run. He died at his beautiful home, Muizeburg, 12 miles from Cape Town in 1940 aged 75.

Probably intrigued by the racing success of his great friend and Rand associate Jack Barnato Joel, Sir Abe started owning horses in this country. Jeol was a good friend to Sir Abe on the Turf – but once the South African's hastiness in rejecting a fine gesture from his friend proved a blow to this country's bloodstock breeding interests. After Lycaon had run third in Sunstar's Guineas and second in Prince Palatine's St Leger, Joel offered this colt to Sir Abe for £10,000. Before the deal was completed Lycaon fell on the road and injured both forelegs. Joel at once cut the price to £8,000. Although the South African wanted the horse for his stud and not to race, he backed out of the deal. A German buyer stepped in – and Lycaon got hundreds of winners in Europe. For over half a century Sir Abe was one of the most powerful personalities in South African public life – and on the British Turf. He notched his first racing success in South Africa when Pomeroy scored in 1887. His first winner in England was Gazeteer who easily beat a big field to land the 1895 Summer Handicap at Hurst Park – and a nice gamble. Although Sir Abe won an Oaks and two Ascot Gold Cups, the best racer to carry his famous black and gold colours was Son-in-Law. The colt was heavily backed to win the 1915 Cesarewitch, when he beat

30 runners with great ease. This was the biggest field to start for the Newmarket marathon for 40 years, and shouldering 8st 4lb Son-in-Law won in then record time.

The millionaire owner is thought to have won about £100,000 when Son-in-Law landed th 1914 Goodwood Cup and Jockey Club Cup. He must have doubled that pick-up over the Newmarket triumph and Son-in-Law went on to win the Jockey Club Cup again in 1915. At Stud Son-in-Law sired countless brilliant winners. These included Foxlaw, who won Sir Abe the 1927 Ascot Gold Cup; the 1924 Oaks victress Straitlace; Boswell, successful in the 1936 St Leger; Trimdon, who landed Ascot Gold Cups in 1931 and 32 . . . . and many others. Sir Abe won the Gold Cup again as an owner with Tiberius — a 500 guineas yearling buy. At Ascot, too, he landed the 1909 Royal Hunt Cup and a hefty gamble with Dark Ronald. Sir Abe was, however, frequently inclined to over-rate the merit of his racehorses. This caused not only disappointment but hefty gambling losses. Ramtapa was a notable example. According to this owner's reckoning the colt was so well tried that he was a certainty for the St Leger. The three-year-old was backed accordingly, but ran nowhere — and, indeed, never showed any merit on the racecourse. There was a consolation prize. At the July Sales in 1929 Sir Abe bought a mare in foal for 950 guineas. The foal was Cecil who won the Alexandra Stakes at Ascot, the Goodwood Cup, the Newbury Cup and dead-heated for the Coronation Cup. Then Cecil ran second to Precipitation in the 1937 Ascot Gold Cup. Here was one betting money-spinner.

His biggest stroke of sale-ring luck, though, followed the 1934 Dublin Sales. Trainer Harry Cottrill bought Lovely Rosa and Dan Bulger there for 710 guineas. He sold the pair to another patron of his stable. Later this man changed his mind, and Cottrill offered the youngsters to Sir Abe, who wrote out the necessary cheque. Throughout his long racing career the South African had strived to win a classic. For 40 years he found Dame Fortune against him. The nearest he got to this goal was winning the 1928 Irish St Leger with Law Suit and owning Robin Goodfellow second to Bahram in the 1935 Derby. Lovely Rosa achieved him his lifetime's ambition by winning the 1936 Oaks at 33-1. Such a long starting price clearly indicated that Sir Abe had not plunged on his filly. When Dan Bulger won the Cambridgeshire that Autumn the bookmakers did not have such a lucky escape. The plunges on this colt were among the heaviest this century. Led by Sir Abe, every professional gambler and commissioner in the business wagered dauntlessly on Dan Bulger. The layers reeled when the three-year-old gave Tommy Weston an arm-chair winning ride — and some accounts were not settled for a while.

Sir Abe had earlier landed Cambridgeshires with Brown Prince (1917) and Raymond (1933) — but this Cesarewitch luck was not always so good as in Son-in-Law's year. In 1921 he backed Tishy to win £200,000. Trained for the South African by Reg Day at Newmarket, Tishy started 6-1 joint favourite for the marathon, but crossed her legs early in the race, lost all interest and dropped out of the running. She did not reach the paddock until most of her rivals had been unsaddled, and was later found to have a temperature — not nearly so high as Sir Abe's, surely. Sir Abe sent Tishy and a big batch of his horses to the December Sales. The filly was bought by James de Rothschild for 1,100 guineas, and prepared specially for the 1922 Cesarewitch. Again she was the medium of a hefty gamble — and again she finished tailed off last.

After winning the 1919 Gimcrack Stakes at York with Southern, Sir Abe showed his wisdom as a Turf reformer. In his speech at the annual Gimcrack dinner he strongly advocated that horses should not be disqualified unless they had interfered with the whole field. This sentiment has been frequently argued since.

Sir Abe won the Gimcrack twice more — with Roral (1929) and Golden Sovereign (1937). His best season was 1936 when his black and gold colours were carried successfully in races worth £24,066. The years 1935 (£23,279) and 1937 (£23,074) were also successful, and during his racing spell in Britain Sir Abe won more than 400 races worth £295,259. His frequent dispersal sales realised huge sums, too. In 1928 he sold his studs and string with the exception only of Son-in-Law and Foxlaw. This was a sudden and unexpected decision. The first 58 lots – including 19 yearlings – from the studs were auctioned for 37,435 guineas. The 39 horses in training made 47,825 guineas. Then in December the remaining 54 mares and foals were sold for 84,560 guineas.

After the tycoon's death the Turf empire had again to be broken up. This time there were 83 lots under the hammer, but prices in 1940 were wartime poor and only 43,077 guineas were realised. When you consider these figures – and realise that Sir Abe bred the winners of 194 races worth £99,945 between 1912 and 1940 – the scale of the South African's race interests can readily be appreciated. In his homeland – where he spent at least six months of every year – Sir Abe won every race of importance. He exported many horses from Britain to South Africa, so boosting the standard of sport there. Racing may not have been beneficial for Sir Abe's pocket. But this effervescent owner certainly enjoyed himself on the Turf – and was good for the business, too.

Certainly one of the heaviest gamblers I ever knew was the Yorkshireman, Charlie Hannam. Railway clerk . . . . smalltime bookmaker . . . . sensational gambler. These were the steps taken by "Old England" who rocked the ring many times. He was called "the most successful gambler of all time" – but failed to settle his losses in the end. Born near Harrogate in 1868 Hannam once lost £50,000 in a week at Ascot. And he paid within a few days. Often he had £5,000 on one race, played billiards for £1,000 a game – and once lost £10,000 to "Bet You a Million" Gates when beaten in a game of darts. Yet this Prince of plungers failed to meet his liabilities and never went onto a racecourse again after losing some £36,000 over Domaha's defeat in the Cambridgeshire.

Charles Hannam was brilliant with figures. He started

making a small book while a junior clerk in a railway office. He made money and in the 1880s this teenager quit his job and took a pitch in Tattersalls. Soon he tired of being a layer and turned punter. During his career trying to beat the bookmakers, Hannam was up every day soon after dawn. His breakfast was light, and he then drank only milk and soda. Form research completed, he had a more substantial meal and set off for the course. His aim was to arrive there at midday, so that he could meet colleagues and glean information.

Not that Hannam took notice of stable gossip. His judgement of horses and races was extremely accurate, and he always relied implicitly on his own interpretation of form. Also Hannam always tried to manipulate his Turf investments by taking advantage of the best odds offered. He had an extraordinary aptitude for figures, and could tell at a glance if odds offered made it possible for him to back several horses and still make a profit if any of them won. Charlie was a great believer in the skill of Sir Gordon Richards. No matter how many horses he backed in a race, he never neglected the champion hockey's mount. He would bet in thousands when others would hesitate to venture more than £100, and was always firm in his opinion. At Newmarket in 1925 he lost more than £10,000 "in one hand" because he did not consider any horse capable of beating Pharos or St Germans in the March Stakes. It was during the 1930s, though, when he won so much money from the ring that he was first termed the "most successful gambler of all time." He certainly amassed a large fortune, and owned a dozen horses. He invested wisely in wool dyeing companies at Bradford and also bought many shares in racecourses.

By this time Hannam was a powerful, influential and most respected man. This multiplied the Turf surprise when he was ordered to leave the York County Stand in 1930. Apparently a "professional gambler" was then taboo in this prim and prissy club. The victim of the insult behaved with considerably more dignity and courtesy then the York officials. He refused to comment on his dismissal – except to say that he was perfectly content to make money in Tattersalls. There are many other much happier stories about "Old England". Charles Morton, the great trainer told me: "For forty years he and I have been acquainted. Charles, like Tennyson's famous brook, seems to go on for ever. Alone of all the thousands of men who have tried to get a fortune backing horses, he has stood the test of time and successfully defied the innumerable attempts to send him into that abyss into which most of the plucky plungers ultimately fall. Most of the big men come to grief in a strange way. They blindly follow the advice of trainers and jockeys, and in the long run discover that success can only be sustained by the men possessing a strong independent judgement . . . . Charles Hannam stands out among the great backers of all time, infinitely preferring his own opinion of a horse to that of the trainer or the owner.

"None of the American betting men were particularly sound in their methods. I entertain clear recollection of a picturesque individual kown as Riley Grannan. He came over here in the nineties with the intention of breaking all the bookmakers in the country. Instead, the boot was very much on the other foot. He had thousands of pounds to bet with, but he was sufficiently shrewd to realise before long that he had no chance. He said that he had come to England because he could not bet enough in America. His bluff was soon called here. Grannan soon went under. He lasted a year or two and then took the knock, owing the ring thousands of pounds. They called him a big better, but compared with Charlie Hannam he was nothing. Even Grannan himself admitted that. 'Gee,' he remarked to me at Newmarket one day, 'Hannam bets more in a week that I would bet in a whole year.' This was perfectly true. Hannam is the greatest and most successful backer of horses that I have ever seen."

Not only of horses. Morton also recalled: "I think that the secret of his success is his iron resolution. You cannot make him deviate one inch from his own opinion. I remember him playing pyramids at Monte Carlo. He was always a good player, especially when there was money at stake. There were bets all round the room, everybody fancying that Hannam was sure to be beaten. The two men went on playing and Hannam was losing £3,000. 'Now' he said 'I will play you double or quits.' Hannam's opponent potted the first six balls, and it seemed to be 100-1 against Old England. But he won, without turning a hair, proof positive of the fact that his nerves are like steel. I do not know another man in the world who could have done it. I have seen all the billiard champions of England get beaten at the Victoria Club in heavy betting games by some of the worst players who have held a cue. Neither they, nor anyone else, can stand the strain of a smoke laden room when bets are being bandied about pell-mell across the table, and hundreds of pounds are betted on every stroke. Charlie Hannam is the single exception. Nothing excites him. Nothing worries him. He will wager £1,000 on making a losing hazard as unemotionally as he will have £5,000 on a horse."

Morton was also prophetic. "I think that he will be the last of the great plungers. Year by Year the tendency is for gambling to become smaller." Throughout his Turf career Hannam believed more in the importance of accurate judgement and correct calculation of odds, than in the whimsiness of luck. And luck was certainly absent in Domaha's Cambridgeshire. Ridden by Gordon Richards, Domaha was drawn 28 of 29 — yet was beaten only two heads. Gordon thought that he won.

The following week Hannam failed to meet his £36,000 losses, and was never seen on a racecourse again. After the death of her 88-year-old father at Harrogate in June 1947, Miss Kathleen Hannam said: "He had a genius for studying form, and his mathematics were amazing. I helped him as his private secretary for many years. Had he stopped betting bfore 1936 he would have been a really rich man." As it was Hannam, whose turnover grew to more than £1,000,000 a year, left £17,000.

Alex Bird has made a fortune backing horses — yet always insists that he is not a gambler — certainly not betting in the sometimes reckless style of the three others I knew well — Charles Hannam, Bob Sievier or Sir Abe Bailey. "I am really a bit of a coward as far as gambling is concerned" Alex told me once. "I have a mortal fear of losing what I have gained by my investments, and this has always been predominant in my mind. Perhaps had I pressed my luck when the market was really strong, I might easily have won a fantastic fortune. I am, however, a family man and I settled for a modest fortune. My investments were far in excess of £1,000,000 a year just after the war, but the market grew weaker over the years and there was little point in continuing with stakes of that magnitude because by doing so one ceases to get value. Indeed, because of the deterioration in the market on the racecourses, it would be folly to continue to bet on a similar scale to that I have done in the past. Nowadays I confine my larger investments to the major meetings such as Chester (May), Epsom (Summer), Royal Ascot, Goodwood (July) and York (August) where I can get some kind of value. If I attend other meetings I do so purely on a social basis. To say that I was shocked at the weakness of the market at a small meeting, would be putting it mildly. One Tattersalls bookmaker, a man who would a few years ago have layed a horse to lose a four-figure amount, refused to lay a horse to win £100, saying 'you have got it to win £80.' This understandably does mean that there will be no more gamblers on a substantial scale."

The son of a bookmaker, Alex has always looked to racing for pleasure and income. He has been a successful owner, winning the 1952 Ebor (Signification), three Ayr Gold Cups with Vatellus (1952), Orthopaedic (1954) and Precious Heather (1956), and many other races. Alex, who never visits casinos, never plays cards — except a family game of bridge — has often flown from Manchester to south country meetings on successive days without making a bet. When photo-finishes were first introduced, he realised that excellent use could be made of the time that it initially took to process negatives. He took up a position on the line, and used his eyes. If he judged that a horse on the far side had won he made no bet. An optical illusion prompts the public in general to think that the horse on the far side has scored – so there was no "market". There was, however no limit to his stake if he thought that the near horse had its nose in front. He once bet £50,000 to win £5,000, and again £60,000 to win £1,000 with William Hill. Often it took five minutes for the photograph to be developed, and Alec used every second to place his money. He made only one mistake – at Epsom where the finishing line is very deceptive – but won well in excess of £100,000 with his successful wagers.

Alex's gamble over the 1954 Grand National has its place in Turf lore. He recalls: "Bobbie Renton won three races in a row with Tudor Line, and I backed the 'chaser each time. I placed all my winnings on Tudor Line for the Grand National, and backed the horse from 40-1 down to 100-8. On the day of the race I had another big bet, and as I climbed the stands to watch the race, I stood to win £275,000 – which would have been the biggest single win on any one horse by one backer in the history of racing." But this was not to be – the horse failed by a neck to catch Royal Tan. Tudor Line had a habit of going out to the right round corners. To prevent this a "pricker" was used in his three races before Aintree. It was left off in the National, and he ran very wide as he entered the straight.

The Grand National has, however, been a lucky race for Alex, who says: "The odds are good, the market is strong and the field can be narrowed down to a small number guaranteed to jump the course." In 1938 he had his first successful tilt at the ring when he backed Battleship at 40-1 with all his available money – £10 a win and £1 a place. His first major coup was over Freebooter, whose success at Aintree in 1950 netted him £60,000. Two years later Teal's victory added £70,000 to the kitty.

In 1951 the Teal colours of Harry Lane on Barnes Park prevented success for a £60,000 wager in the Lincolnshire Handicap. Alex had backed his own horse Newton Heath to win this amount, and the miler looked certain to score when the saddle slipped and he went under by half-a-length.

Now Alex, who was five and a half years in the Navy during the Second World War, goes racing more for pleasure than for business. He reckons that betting taxes make it almost impossible to wager sensibly and finds that bookmakers will not strike a sizeable bet anyway.

CHAPTER EIGHT

TRAINERS, JOCKEYS AND OWNERS

In the early days of racing, owners had their horses trained on their home estates by one of their grooms and ridden in their races by local boys. When the benefit of gallops at places like Newmarket, Lambourn, Hambleton, Malton and Middleham were realised, professional trainers appeared on the scene and built ranges of stabling near wide expanses of old turf downland. For some years they were few in number. They were known as "training grooms" and wore the livery of those who employed them. Until men of higher social position entered the ranks of trainers those in the profession were either the sons of trainers or ex-jockeys. They had had a long experience of stable routine and the art, science and mystery of preparing horses for racing. Much of that "art" – the long severe sweating gallops, frequent bleeding, for instance – has long since been discontinued. In due course there came an influx of young men, who had gained experience as premium pupils with prominent trainers. They taught them not only stable management, their own system of readying horses from stage to stage, but also the ever increasing office work associated with the profession. In addition to these, there are now a considerable number of men holding trainer's licences who have had no experience of the routine of a big training establishment before starting their careers. Most of them have had the supervision of, and practical work with, hunters and point-to-pointers so have discovered what feed and what work produces the best results.

There are always new recruits joining the Turf army to take

the place of those who have left the ranks. All the newcomers think they can be more clever than those who have gone before. I have discovered the same conceit in each younger generation of trainers, jockeys and owners. They know all what there is to know about riding, training and racing after a couple of years experience. Some of us have found that after sixty years at the game we are just beginning to learn.

The last time Sir Cecil Boyd-Rochfort and I had a long chat he recalled when we both used to stay with his aunt Maud Cheape, one of the greatest sportswomen England has ever known. In those days her sons Hugh and Leslie Cheape were among the best polo players and horsemen in Great Britain. The other brother Gen. Ronny Cheape, was keener on racing and for a number of years lived near Catterick and ran a lot of horses at North country fixtures. We had great fun at Bentley Manor. The Cheape's had money to burn, a stable full of good horses, and the best of shooting and the jolliest of house-parties. What Sir Cecil emphasised was that we were all very young men then, but we all considered ourselves fully competent to criticise with finality owners, trainers, jockeys, horses, Masters of Hounds and huntsmen. Sir Cecil wound up with the remark, "You and I have found we know a good dea less about horses, training and racing than we thought we did." And Sir Cecil trained for over 40 years! Before he embarked on his career he was for some time with Atty Persse to get a thorough grounding in running a training establishment.

Sir Cecil and I first met when we were both staying with Mrs. Cheape, known to the whole sporting world as "The Squire of Bentley." She had two estates in Scotland, and another at Bentley, in Worcestershire. Sir Cecil and a number of young sportsmen destined to become famous in the racing, hunting, polo and army world, were continually coming and going. Hugh, Leslie and Ronny became generals, and "The Squire" also had three daughters, who all made their mark as horsewomen.

What jolly times we had both on the Isle of Mull and at Bentley! Mrs. Cheape ran her various establishments in the grand fashion. At Bentley she had her own famous pack of harriers and was a great horsewoman, riding with the Worcestershire foxhounds in scarlet. Bentley was run on princely lines. We will never again see such magnificence. There was always the butler and two or three footmen at table, and into 'teens of grooms and stable-helpers for the horses. There were three gamekeepers, and six men regularly employed in the gardens.

Sir Cecil was keen on racing, though I don't think he had then made up his mind to become a trainer. He often came into Yorkshire to hunt and the friendship between us deepened over the years. When we met in the paddocks at race meetings he always recalled the days when we were both young. If Walter Easterby was in the offing, he was roped in to the discussions, because Sir Cecil often visited Walter's father when he hunted in Yorkshire. Walter Easterby trained Ronny Cheape's jumpers. Ronny was a bold horseman and useful across country to hounds, but he did not shine as an amateur jockey, though he had any amount of courage and keenness. He eventually went to live on the family property on the Isle of Mull and died when on a visit to Kenya.

Many of the most prominent owners, trainers and jockeys have begun their sporting career riding across country to hounds. To mention only a few, Willie Stephenson – ex-jockey and now Royston trainer – and his cousin Arthur of Bishop Auckland, both graduated in the hunting field while Bobby Renton, Stewart Wight, Capt. Neville Crump, the brothers Nimrod and "Jumbo" Wilkinson and Walter Easterby all had a similar beginning. Walter's two nephews Miles – always known as Peter – and Michael, are carrying on the training tradition on their respective farms near Malton, and very well they have both done.

There is a long "horsey" background to the family for Walter Easterby's father was at the Stockwell Stud Farm near Tadcaster before him. In 1925 Walter had moved from Yorkshire, where he had ridden lots of point-to-point and steelplechase winners, to become private trainer to the late

Lady Lindsay in Scotland. She was not easy to deal with, and Walter didn't stay long in Scotland. He first started as a public trainer at Catterick and in 1928 moved to Middleham, mainly concerned with the National Hunt game. In 1930 he and his jockey Jack Mason had the hard luck to be beaten in the Liverpool and Scottish Grand Nationals, in both of which their Melleray's Belle was close second. From Middleham Walter Easterby went to Malton and trained a lot of winners at Grove House. In 1948 he took over the Stockwell Stud, named after the mighty Stockwell, who stood there after winning the 1852 Two Thousand Guineas and St Leger. He sired the Derby winners Blair Athol (1864), Lord Lyon (1866) and Doncaster (1873). In Lord Lyon's year his sons were 1, 2 and 3 in the Derby.

In my early days one of the best sportsmen I used to meet was Col. Roly Milvain. Roly lived at Eglingham Hall, near Alnwick, and there trained a few horses and had kennelled the pack bearing his name which he hunted at his own expense for over thirty years. For a similar period he rode as an amateur, despite the fact that he was one of the few to live after breaking his neck. He was a prominent figure in the Northern Turf world, particularly at National Hunt meetings, and up to the time of his death in 1960 was chairman of the Rothbury Race Committee. On that curious little course, and at Kelso and Hexham, he rode many winners. Starting his Turf career at the time his friend Col. Percy Bewicke was making rather a stir in the Turf world, Roly lived to be eighty and we often recalled the old days when Percy Bewicke was riding a lot of winners and betting heavily.

Of all the members of the ancient Bewicke family — one of them was Mayor of Newcastle 500 years ago — the one whose name stands out most prominently in Turf annals is Capt. Percy Wentworth Bewicke. He died in 1950 at the age of 89, and left his considerable fortune to his great-nephew Major Calverly Bewicke who trains at Didcot in Oxfordshire and won the 1958 Cheltenham Gold Cup with Kerstin before moving

South. All the Bewickes have been horsemen and horsewomen, and Capt. Percy was the leading amateur rider for 1890-2. A 15th Hussar officer, he won the Military Gold Cup on Omerod, twice rode the winner of the Grand Hurdle at Auteuil and four times rode in the Grand National. On leaving the service he was the leading spirit in a confederacy closely associated with John Powney's Grately stable. They brought off a number of coups which shook the ring.

One of these was with Little Eva,which ran in the name of another 15th Hussar officer (Capt. Bald), and won the 1901 Lincolnshire Handicap at 100-15. This was an epoch of heavy wagering, and the Grately Confederacy, won a great amount of money with this coup. In 1905 Capt. Bewicke took out a trainer's licence and had stables at Belsay, a Northumbrian estate rich in Turf and stud tradition. Hugh Powney left his brother and Grately to become his assistant. There were many merry days and nights in Northumberland at that time, for the country was full of young sportsmen with good horses, the ability to ride them both in silk and scarlet, and all caught with the gambling fever. Capt. Bewicke was their mentor and among his contemporaries and close friends were the Strakers, Roly Milvain, the Pawsons, Adam Scott, C. W. C. Henderson — who owned Hexham racecourse — J. S. Fawcus — father of the former Middleham trainer — Addy Cresswell and Alex Brown, of Calally Castle.

Well do I remember Capt. Bewicke's last ride as an amateur. It was at the Hexham 1910 May meeting. He rode the 7-1 on certainty Herbert Vincent, owned by Fred Straker, in the Tynedale flat race, and was pipped at the post by Jim Storie on his useful old horse Calliope. Capt. Bewicke wore an immaculate white hunting stock which made movement of his head difficult, and Jim Storie, stealing up to his blind side, beat him a head. The captain was furious, and I can see him now throw his saddle down in the weighing room saying he would never ride another race. A few days later Herbert Vincent won by eight lengths at Uttoxeter with Bob Chadwick riding. Capt. Bewicke soon moved to Newmarket where he trained until 1927. After that I don't think that he ever set foot on a racecourse again, but retired to Scotland where he played golf and salmon fished.

There is now another trainer Powney, the son of Mr. & Mrs. John Powney of Bury Road, Newmarket. John jnr was one of David Robinson's private trainers for a couple of seasons, and now has his own yard. His great-grandfather John started to train in 1849 on the family property near Bath racecourse — Powneys had owned land there since 1600. He married a niece of the famous John Day and they jointly owned the famous Cup horse The Hero. From Bath the Powneys moved to Durrington, Wilts, where John Powney II trained for many years. He too, had a long association with the Grately stable, as did his brother Harry, a successful jockey. Hugh went with Sir John Renwick to Whitewall, Malton in 1909 and later trained on his own account at Hambleton. On leaving Hambleton Hugh went as private trainer to Sir E. Cassel, and later trained — with Sir Cecil Boyd Rochfort as manager — for Marshall Field. Sir Cecil soon took complete control of the horses, though.

Also associated with Capt. Bewicke in the North was the late Jack Weymes, whose son Ernest, succeeded him at Tupgill, Middleham in 1958. Jack Weymes always interested me a lot. He had such a colourful career before he became a successful steeplechase jockey after the First World War. He never served his apprenticeship but had some years with the astute Capt. Bewicke when he was training in Northumberland. Then he went to Australia where he rode buck-jumping broncos and also competed in steeplechases. On his return home Adam Scott engaged him as stable jockey and afterwards he was with Stewart Wight. Then he became private trainer to Frank Usher, and afterwards was associated with Capt. Fawcus's stable at Middleham until he started to train.

Norman Bertie, is one of several Northumbrians who have made their mark on the Turf. Among the others are the

Watsons – so long trainers for the Rothschild family after leaving Richmond, Yorkshire – the Bullocks, – trainers and jockeys for three generations, who hailed originally from Morpeth and were long located at Newcastle and Joe Lawson. Norman, who retired from training when another Northumbrian, Jack Clayton, took over Bedford House stable as trainer, was born at Wallsend and educated at Rutherford College, Newcastle. He served his apprenticeship with Sam Darling, and for many years was head man for Fred Darling. On Darling retiring in 1947 Bertie succeeded him and later went to Newmarket where he had Royal patrons. He will best be remembered as trainer of the 1953 Derby winner Pinza, and Belle of All, winner of the 1951 1,000 Guineas. Sir Gordon Richards scored his only Derby triumph on Pinza and also rode Belle of All.

My old friend Hewitt Henry Golightly must have been one of the oldest trainers holding a licence. A Derbyshire man, born in 1881, he began his Turf career in Yorkshire. After having a few horses with George Gunter at Wetherby – Clara B was his first – he set up as a public trainer at Barlow, near Selby in 1920. His first winner was Dropitin, owned by George Picken who was the chairman of the Northern Bookmakers' Protection Association. George, who retired to Epsom, was in those days a prominent man on the Northern Turf. His father had been a Teesside bookmaker and George, after being an amateur sprinter and boxing promoter, switched his attention to the Turf. Always very outspoken he once startled an influential sporting gathering by saying, "If the Jockey Club does not wake up to its responsibilities, the time is fast approaching when there will be a breakaway. Racing clubs will come into being to control sport in their own area. They will do it one more up-to-date and democratic lines than at present." That by the way was 55 years ago.

Picken and Golightly were robbed of Ebor honours in 1926. Pat Donoghue, son of Steve, rode Dropitin and about two furlongs from home was hit in the eye by a thrown-up stone.

He was a blind passenger for the remainder of the distance and did not know when the winning-post was reached. Sol Joel's Pons Asinorum, who was the favourite, won by three-quarters of a length, Seradella was second and Dropitin a short-head away was third. Golightly was originally a mining engineer but in the First World War turned his attention to building airplanes at Selby. In 1929 his gallops were requisitioned and he moved to Hoofprints, Coombe Bissett, Salisbury, where he trained until a few years ago. Golightly was fortunate in that his head man was "Darky" Cooper — father of the former Malton trainer, Albert Cooper — who came to him from George Gunter.

"Darky" was at Coombe Bissett for twenty-two years. Among the races Golightly won when in Yorkshire was the coveted Watt Memorial Plate at Beverley. The horse was Passing Cloud, owned by J. W. Hallett of Sheffield. It was the sportsman's first winner, and seeing his flame jacket with Kingfisher blue sleeves flash past the post so excited him that he was seized with a violent attack of diarrhoea and could not be found when the plate was to be presented to him in the stewards' room. It was assumed that he was in the champagne bar — but he wasn't! His trainer deputised for him as he made himself more "comfortable" behind the stands.

William Binnie, who also trained at Malton, was another old friend with whom I travelled thousands of miles to attend race meetings. We usually journeyed by train to Scotland together before the days of cars, and he was a most interesting and well-informed companion. I learned a lot from him. He was the third generation to train and, like several others, left Scotland for Yorkshire and was first based at Middleham. William Binnie was born in 1863 and died in 1937, his son Billy taking over the stable, and with it that grand old horse Mount Lothian, which won so many races and was a Pontefract specialist. William often told me that he hated to watch a race in which he had a fancied runner, especially — as was often the case — if he had put the money down to some tune. He was quick-tempered and allowed no one to dictate to him, or take any liberties. A most astute man, no one could weigh up form better, or keep his own counsel closer. He was a bit of an artist with a passion for painting Napoleon. I remember the days when he had a pack of beagles. Charlie Ringstead, who became one of the best jockeys in the North, was then an apprentice to him and used to come out on a pony to whip in. Occasionally John Brown of Marton Common, Kirbymoorside, had Binnie and the beagles over. He always invited me to stay on these days and provided a horse for me. We were jumping fences all day long and then made a night of it. Capt. Watson Cameron was one of the patrons of Binnie's stable. He also had horses with Bob Armstrong at Penrith. One of the best horses Mr. Cameron had with Binnie was Isabelle II, who won races each season at Sedgefield, Catterick, Cartmel and in Scotland from 1906 onwards. Tommy Raine was always the jockey. I saw this game old mare win most of her races and particularly recall her beating Capt. Paynter's Aquador at the final 1911 Doncaster National Hunt meeting – jumping was not revived there until 1946. The Captain, a week or two afterwards, had his revenge at Wetherby when he beat the odds-on Isabelle. Incidentally Capt. Cameron's grandson, Tony Cameron, rode a brilliant race when finishing fourth in the 1962 Grand National. The West Hartlepool brewer was one of those responsible for reviving Hartlepool Races in 1890. The meeting however, lasted only a couple of years.

George Gunter trained a lot of winners on his father's estate at Wetherby with the aid of Bob Harper and "Darky" Cooper. George Gunter was more than once top of the amateur riders' list and rode his first winner, on April 1, 1899. He was then at Cirencester Agricultural College, where he had gone from Eton. Disabled by sciatica, the result of racecourse falls, and being mauled by a savage stallion, he still raced at Wetherby – where he rode so many winners – when in his 80s. He went on race riding until he was 56. We used to see a lot of each other in the early years of this century and I remember well one visit to him at Wetherby about 1910. He had asked me if I could sell for him a couple of stallions with which he had been winning 'chases but which were getting on a bit in years. John Brown was wanting a thoroughbred stallion to get hunters, so I took him to Wetherby to see the two George Gunter had for sale. We went to one box and found the occupant racked up short, ears back, whites of eyes showing, and a hind leg uplifted ready to lash out. That was sufficient for John Brown, who merely remarked "Let's see t'other." When Bob Harper opened the second box door we were greeted by a screaming horse with open mouth ready to seize hold of anyone who entered. Despite Bob Harper's assurance that it was only high spirits and play the Yorkshire hunter breeder said: "Shut him up! I've seen quite enough! I want a stallion likely to win a premium and getting hunters, not a bloody lion!"

A fascinating paddock personality of this era was the Turf "Jack-of-all-trades" J. A. Whipp, who started life as a farmer near Beverley, later became an owner and bookmaker, and latterly a trainer. He died in 1922. One of the best horses he had was Tommy Tittlemouse for which he paid 110 guineas after a selling race at Haydock Park. Tommy Tittlemouse ran in 171 races, won 41 of them, and was the last horse Fred Archer ever rode.

I was very friendly with Percy Botterill. After training at Doncaster for a few years he went to Malton in 1911, where he continued until things became too difficult during the Second World War. At the end of hostilities he told me he felt like a fish out of water without any horses but he never started again and left Malton for Scarborough. He and Capt. Elsey were lads together in Lincolnshire, where both their fathers bred and trained bloodstock. One of the first horses Percy trained was a hunter, Highland, bred by his father, which he had ridden with the South Lincs Hounds and found had a wonderful turn of speed. So he should have had for he was by The Lambkin out of Lowland Maid. After winning over hurdles and some hunter flat races in 1895 Highland was entered in handicaps on the flat and won the first of them at Liverpool, and six more the same season, always with top weight. I remember the veteran ex-trainer telling me that when Highland (8st 4lb) beat Argonaut (7st 1lb) in the Autumn Handicap at Birmingham in 1895, Joe Cannon said to him, "I have 40 horses in my stable and not one of them can give Argonaut 21 lb but you have done it with a hunter!" Seven handicaps always with top weight in one season must be a record for a hunter.

Percy's son Jack, decided there was more money and less worry in selling horses than training them. He not only had his successful Ascot Bloodstock Sales but acted as auctioneer at a considerable number of meetings in the North and Midlands. His death in May 1962 came as a great shock. His son Michael, who joined him after being with Goffs' in Dublin continues the Ascot Sales.

A trainer I knew well and liked a lot was Cecil Ray, who trained at Malton until his licence was withdrawn in 1946. I always thought he was more sinned against than sinning. Cecil was born in Kent but served his apprenticeship in South Africa, where he rode over 700 winners, before coming home to ride. He was a clever jockey, and equally skilful as a trainer. What is more he was a real horse lover. I have in my possession letters he wrote me after losing his licence, which go to show how bitterly he felt what he considered a heart-breaking injustice. Heart-breaking it actually was for poor Cecil, who lived only a couple of years afterwards, his death at the age of 55 taking place at Ewell, near Epsom in 1948. When he lost his licence he begged me to take two of his stable favourites, Stretto, the winner of the Stockton Handicap; and Hernani, the winner of the Thirsk Handicap. He wanted to ensure them and affectionate home to the end of their days. I realised that the future of these two horses was one of the many worries on his mind and I agreed that they should have one of my paddocks in the summer and a couple of loose-boxes in bad weather. I kept my promise and Stretto and Hernani ("Bobbie" as he was called) soon became beloved members of our family. I think the following extracts from my diary regarding their respective ends will show how Cecil's stable pets had become our equine friends. February 19, 1948: "Nothing seemed more certain than that Stretto (son of the Derby and St Leger winner Coronach) would win me some races this spring and give my son Noel his first winning ride as an amateur over hurdles. Six weeks ago Stretto had an accident, poison got into his ankle joint, and he has been standing on three legs in pain. I personally poulticed and spent hours fermenting with hot water, but all to no avail. The hitherto proud, not very sweet-tempered or easy to deal with Stretto became as quiet as a lamb, as confiding and trustful as a pet dog, but wonderfully gallant in all his pain. At last the vet and I decided that the kindest thing was to end the horse's misery. I got the assurance from the Cleveland kennels, that the old horse would be put down with the humane killer immediately on arrival. So ended the career of an imperious, high couraged, blue-blooded winner of many races. Only in his latter days of suffering was he really lovable, although always a great favourite with Cecil.

Latterly he licked my hand and looked at me with those big pathetic eyes as though to beg me to give him ease — and how hard I tried! I will mourn him to the end of my days. Poor, dear old Stretto! His end was a sporting one as was his whole life."

Here is my diary record of the passing of Hernani two years later: "This morning when I went to Bobbie's box with his corn there was no welcoming whinny I was shocked to find him laid dead. He was as fit as a fiddle when I had ridden him the previous morning. He had whinnied for his supper, and eaten it all. I shut him up for the night and he gave me his usual lick when I patted him and left him eating his hay. I could only put death down to a heart attack, but a vet held a post mortem and thought it possible poor little Bobbie had gone to sleep standing, had dropped down when sleeping, and a hoof had burst an intestine. He was not old, and I think he was the most lovable and affectionate of the many horses I have had and loved. I always looked after Bobbie myself, dressed him over and rode him, and never a night passed but my wife took him a tit-bit of some sort, for which he regularly waited with his head over the half-door of his box.

"Those who become attached to their horses, who talk to them and treat them like the pals they are, will understand how sad we are at the death of poor Bobbie. Now I have nothing I can ride, for I am getting too old to mount young 'uns. This may mean the end of my riding, which all through my life has been one of my greatest joys. Or will I find some old blood 'un to put into Bobbie's box? . . . . Not for some little time, and even then, he can never win the place in my heart Bobbie had. He leaves a sweet memory behind him as well as a heart-break!"

That was twenty-five years ago. I never rode again and have sadly missed the happiness and carefree wonder that comes immediately a horse lover slips boots into stirrups.

For years, the Darlington, Richmond and Piercebridge localities have produced first-class trainers, jockeys, point-to-point and amateur riders under rules. Many of us remember Jack Hett of Piercebridge, who for so many years was one of the main supporters of the jumping meetings at Sedgefield, Catterick, Shincliffe and Wetherby as owner, trainer and jockey. I fancy that it was he who put the idea of becoming a jockey into the head of Ernie Davey, the Malton trainer, who spent his boyhood at Piercebridge Hall where Hett trained.

After Redcar races in 1974 I had a call from Ernie, who I have known almost from the start of his racing career. This was not only a friendly visit but also one of enquiry. Ernie wanted to find the date of his first ride as a steeplechase jockey. He knew it was on Irish Oak at Cheltenham. We found the date was May 15, 1912. Captain Beatty won the race on The Chemist and Davey was third. He went to Ireland soon after the Cheltenham ride and was there for eight years, riding on every course in Eire. He returned to this country and joined Capt. Darby Rogers at Sparsholt. After a season or so Capt. Gooch engaged him as steeplechase jockey. Then Davey started as a trainer at Sparsholt and was there for five years. He came back to his native North country in 1925 and threw in his lot with Billy Bellerby, who had just taken the Hambleton training quarters. Ernie continued to ride a lot as a steeplechase jockey, but in his first few months at Hambleton was mainly responsible for training King of Clubs to win the 1926 Lincolnshire Handicap for the Bellerby stable. King of Clubs won at 100-1 and was ridden by Pat Donoghue. Soon after Ernie went to Dumfermline as private trainer to John Johnstone — father of Andrew Johnstone of Brickfields Stud. He was with Mr. Johnstone until 1933 and after a short time as private trainer to W. Webster, he bought the Star Farm training quarters at Malton and developed his own splendid gallops, which never get hard in the dryest summer. He never used Langton Wold, as do all other Malton trainers, except Bill Elsey, who also has his private gallops at Highfield. Ernie's son Paul, was David Robinson's most successful ever trainer. Speaking of Paul, Ernie often told me, "They used to say I was a fairly good judge when buying at sales, but Paul has proved himself better." Paul married a daughter of that very clever trainer Walter Pollock, who was born at Hull and apprenticed to the Hon. George Lambton, with whom he remained for 25 years before starting training at Malton.

Many of our trainers are the third, fourth and fifth generation to continue family tradition. The Days, Darlings, Waughs, Jarvis's, Rickabys, Vaseys, Binnies, Armstrongs, Peacocks, Watsons, Leaders and Elseys are all examples.

Charles Elsey, the son of William Elsey, has been followed at Highfield by his son Bill. At Baumber in Lincolnshire William once trained 300 winners during a three year spell and in 1893 saddled a record 123 winners. Charles won 1,500 races including the Two Thousand Guineas (Neurula 1953) the One Thousand Guineas (Musidora 1949 and Honeylight 1956) the Oaks (Musidora and Frieze 1952) and the St Leger (Cantello 1959). He was champion trainer in 1956 when he notched 83 successes worth £61,621.

When Charles Elsey retired, Bill became the third generation in the Elsey training saga. Among other characteristics he has inherited from his father and grandfather is absolute frankness about horses under his charge: never giving equine ducks long necks so that they masquerade as swans. I often heard grandfather William Elsey say, after being questioned by information-hunters, "I always tell them the truth, for when you do that people don't believe you." Once I remember him telling an inveterate paddock pest: "My horse is fit and well, and he's trying. Now you know as much as I do."

Charles and I began our Turf careers at the same time and were friends all our lives. Charles often talked to me of his son Bill, and for a short time regretted that he was more keen on aeroplanes than on horses. Bill thought the Turf too down to earth and dull. He had his head in the clouds — as a pilot. Echoing the best fairy stories, though, the Turf turned to gold for Bill too and during his career he has won the Oaks with Pia in 1967 and the St Leger with Peleid six years later. Since taking control of Highfield in 1960 he has trained some 600 winners of £500,000 stakes. He is undoubtedly as brilliant as his grandfather and father.

Yet Bill certainly rated aeroplanes better than horses for many years. He was all set to serve an apprenticeship in the horse training art with Joe Lawson when the Second World War broke out. At once he volunteered for the RAF and flew Hurricanes and Typhoons in India, Burma, Persia, North Africa and Germany.

After demobilisation Bill spent a year at the Royal Agricultural College, Cirencester, before joining Noel Murless — then at Beckhampton — as pupil. He was due to stay two years but left after six months to become a ferry pilot. Bill remained a civil pilot during the Berlin airlift, and had 3,500 flying hours logged when he settled on the Turf again in 1952. Bill joined his father in the management of Highfield and had a hand in the preparation of most of the stable's classic triumphs. He is a very astute trainer, and a tireless worker. Bill

PLATE 7
Three famous personalities. Dobson and Matt Peacock share a bench with bowler-hatted Mr. Lionel Dugdale.

PLATE 8
Talking with Edgar Britt *(left)* and Jim Adams *(centre)*, the author enjoys a day at Redcar Races in 1951.

PLATE 9

Senior Steward of the National Hunt Committee, John Rogerson *(centre)* shares a joke with the author and Wing Commander Peter Vaux *(right)* at Catterick in 1959.

PLATE 10

At Hexham in 1959. *(Left to right)* Seth Smith (Starter), W. Patterson (Secretary) and the author (Clerk of Scales).

is devoted to his horses, and has recently started to run some of his older charges over hurdles too. I was delighted to note his first success, achieved when Mark Henry won at Newcastle in December 1975.

Dick Peacock has followed his grandfather, Dobson, and father, Matt, at the Manor House, Middleham. A wartime Scots Greys officer, Dick spent his boyhood learning stable management from Matt — who won the wartime Derby with Dante in 1945 and so is the most recent Northern trainer of a Derby winner. When Matt died in 1951, Dick took over the stable and his first winner was Helewise — a present to him from his father. Since then he has saddled Precast to take the 1954 Gimcrack Stakes, Lindsay to win the Cheveley Park Stakes in 1958 and Sweet Story to triumph in the 1966 Northumberland Plate. Dick also manages his own stud, and breeds many of the horses that he trains.

Steve Donoghue ran away from his Warrington home in 1900 and tackled Dobson Peacock in the paddock at Stockton races. The Middleham trainer was struck with the confidence and boldness of the little lad and offered to take him as an apprentice. Unfortunately, Steve, having bolted from Warrington, gave his name as Steve Smith. Being told soon after his arrival at Middleham that census papers had to be filled in for all the employees at Middleham's Manor House stables, Steve feared his fictitious name would be discovered. Not having been actually apprenticed, he slipped away one night — so Yorkshire missed the distinction of producing a great jockey. Steve was apprenticed to John Porter at Kingsclere, but ran away again — this time to France where he rode his first winner (Hanoi) in 1905 at the age of 19. He went to Ireland and headed the jockey's list in 1909. Steve's first mount in England was Christine at Liverpool in 1908, and his first winner was Golden Rod on the same course in July the following year. He was subsequently British Champion 10 times and his 14 classic successes included six Derbys. He retired in 1937 and died in 1945.

Sir Gordon Richards then assumed Donoghue's championship mantle, and wore the crown 25 times.

What always struck me most about Sir Gordon was his quiet, unassuming manner. Those of us who spend much of our racing life in weighing-rooms, have an opportunity of seeing and studying jockeys from quite a different angle. It is like being behind the scenes, in the dressing-rooms and wings of a theatre. There actors and actresses, even though dressed and made up, are their natural selves. So it is with jockeys for they look upon the wieghing-room as a sort of refuge and sanctuary in which they are safe from the importuning, questioning, lionising and mobbing of a certain type in the paddock.

I fancy none appreciate the value of the weighing-room in this connection more than Sir Gordon. He never lost his shy, retiring modesty which made excessive limelight and hero-worship rather repugnant. Unlike many of his contemporaries, there was nothing of the boisterous, excitable hurry and whirl in the weighing-room with him, no shouting for his valet, no last-minute dash to the scale, and bull-in-the-china-shop-like tearing back to the dressing-room.

To look at him, as I have done, patiently waiting his turn in the queue to be weighed out, one might imagine he was some obscure lad, not quite sure of the ropes and anxious to keep in the background. In his humility, his good manners and his restraint lay not only much of his power, but also a natural gentlemanliness and gentleness, which have also stood him in good stead. One admires it all, and it has not detracted in any way from his fame. Sir Gordon certainly lacks the mobile face of Steve Donoghue, the charm of Michael Beary — "Angel Face", as he has been called to his own amusement — the humour of Joe Taylor and Willie Nevett, the vivacity of Joe Caldwell, the quaint piquancy of Johnnie Dines, the assurance and domination of Tommy Weston, the supreme confidence of Harry Wragg, the seeming wearied detachment of Rufus Beasley, the business-like haste of Charlie Smirke, the grave matter-of-factness of Joe Childs, the alertness and happiness of Henry Jellis, the brightness of eye and smile of Willie Christie, the fun of Davy McGuigan and the buoyancy of Harry Gunn.

Sir Gordon's face, when in repose, would suggest sadness rather than any of those qualities and attributes possessed by some of his contemporaries. I have never seen him "rattled" and I have rarely seen signs of that strain and weariness which are both so often marked in jockeys who have been wasting hard, who are worn out with travelling and with late nights, depressed by a run of bad luck, or the adverse criticisms of owners or trainers. Sometimes criticism enters like iron into a jockey's heart when he knows such censure is not justified. Sir Gordon and I have had many chats in weighing-rooms and during the course of them I have hardly ever mentioned racing. I fancy it is rather a relief to him to find someone who is not so absolutely single-minded as to have no thought or interest beyond the constant striving to find winners.

His dislike of lionising and vulgar curiosity is obvious. I had a very clear example of this when he came to Thirsk on Friday, November 3, 1933. He told me on that beastly day, one of the few wet afternoons Thirsk has had since the whole course and appointments were reconstructed after the First World War, that he felt "like a hunted fox." It was Captain Stanley "Jack" Wilson who had persuaded Gordon to ride at Thirsk in his attempt to equal Fred Archer's record of 246 winning mounts in one season. The same evening I recorded in my diary:

"A record crowd at Thirsk despite the filthy day. The Press had roused public interest in Gordon Richards to boiling-point and Captain 'Jack' Wilson — who is one of the directors of Thirsk — saw that it would be a great draw to the meeting. Also he was anxious that Richards should achieve his ambition of reaching Archer's record by riding the necessary winner on the Yorkshire course. The Captain had had bills printed and circulated in Leeds, York and elsewhere announcing that the champion jockey would ride at Thirsk (whereas the only time

Fred Archer rode at the meeting, a bell-man was sent round to announce that 'the great Mr. Archer will positively appear at Thirsk this afternoon').

"No doubt this proved a great draw, as did Richards, whose present effort to equal Archer's remarkable figures has so captured the public imagination. Well, he didn't achieve his objective at Thirsk and when he does it cannot be compared with Archer's wonderful total for one season (1885) in view of the difference in the weight of the two men and the much greater number of mounts Richards has had this year in comparison with Archer's total rides in his record year. Gordon motored down from York to Thirsk and in his wake – he had a big advance-guard of them, too – came a crowd of Press photographers, cinematograph men and reporters.

"The camera men would have filled the unsaddling paddock, so could not be allowed there. Eventually they decided that they could snap the triumphal procession from the top of the weighing-room and I was kept busy writing out permits for them to take up their position there. Then press-men came singly and in groups, to see how they could 'get at' Richards for an interview after he had ridden a winner. There were literally dozens of them. The weighing-room was besieged and it was all we could do to keep the attacking army out of the jockey's dressing-room. I went in and had a word with the little man, who was obviously uncomfortable at all the fuss. At first he declined to be interviewed, but I told him that he would be dogged, shadowed and cornered until he did say something to the Press. I suggested that he'd better see one or two of the Press-men in the weighing-room after he had ridden a winner, and let them give the others what he said. To this course he agreed with some reluctance.

"As it turned out, he had a blank day, so there was no interviewing and no cheering. It was an afternoon which I know got on his nerves. A man who is already highly strung, doesn't want all this distinction, mental upheaval and electricity in the air, when he has to ride. He cannot really do his best and he was very glad when it was over, though he will have to go through it again tomorrow at Hurst Park. He'll be hunted there just as he was today at Thirsk. A thousand extra race-cards were printed today and were soon gone. Some men who love being lionised would have thoroughly enjoyed the whole thing — Gordon didn't! I could see that even the invitation he got to go into the private luncheon-rooms in the club stand was not appreciated. He was like a badger being baited and drawn when he wanted to creep away into a corner and be left alone."

The equalling of Fred Archer's record was not long delayed because on the very next day Gordon rode El Senor to win the Mitre Selling Handicap at Hurst Park. Then the storm broke. Photographs of Richards occupied a prominent position in every newspaper, and columns of features were turned out by enthusiastic journalists. He was seen by millions of patrons of picture palaces and was feted wherever he went. Mr. E. Thornton Smith, the owner of El Senor, presented him with Fred Archer's whip and spurs which he had just bought in a London auction room. Jack Turner — whose Ennis Bridge had provided Gordon with his 240th winner — gave him another interesting Archer souvenir in the shape of a china dish, on which was a picture of the immortal "Tinman" together with details of his career. Perhaps the most appreciated of all the gifts he received at this time was the address of welcome and congratulations inscribed on vellum, presented to him by the District Council and sportsmen of his birth-place, Oakengates. The presentation was made by Steve Donoghue at a civic reception at which 300 guests were present, among whom were several of the leading jockeys, Jimmy Wilde the boxer, and Richards' old master, Martin Hartigan. Gordon completed the 1933 season with an astonishing 259 winners. On October 3, 4, and 5 he won 12 races in succession, beginning with one at Nottingham, followed by all six at Chepstow the next day and the first five on the second day. In 1943 he passed Archer's tally of 2,748 winners, and when he retired on August 10, 1954, his amazing total was 4,870 winners from 21,834 mounts.

Jim Adams gave Willie Nevett his first winning ride — on Stockwood in an apprentice race at Carlisle in 1924. I saddled Stockwood and gave Willie the leg-up little thinking that he would be a leading jockey and would win Derbys on Owen Tudor (1941) Ocean Swell (1944) and Dante (1945).

For very many years Willie Nevett was champion jockey in the North. Following that afternoon at Carlisle in 1924 Willie rapidly climbed the Turf ladder. A great jockey, he found his relaxation in gardening. When he lived at Patrick Brompton Hall, near Middleham, he had beautiful and extensive gardens and grounds from which came the sweet peas, gladiolas, roses and vegetables which won so many prizes at North country shows. He learned the art of growing flowers and garden produce by experience and his own hard work and tremendous enthusiasm resulted in him becoming one of the most successful exhibitors in the north, adding to his fame as a jockey. There seemed to be acres of lawns, glass, flowerbeds and kitchen garden and the fact that Willie and one man kept all this in perfect order and grew such wonderful flowers, fruit and vegetables was astonishing.

I once had a most interesting chat with his father — who was with Harry Hall when he trained at Spigot Lodge, Middleham. That was in the days when the late Dobson Peacock was a young man and was riding occasionally for Harry Hall in amateur races. The veteran Mr. Nevett told me that when Spigot Lodge was full up with horses, Hall sent some to Mr. Peacock. That was how the Manor House eventually became a famous and successful training establishment. Dobson Peacock in due course took out a licence as a trainer and built up a powerful connection and stable. When with Harry Hall, Mr. Nevitt tended Why Not when he ran second in the 1889 Grand National, ridden by Mr. Charlie Cunningham, who had to waste so hard to do 11st 5lbs that he was really too weak to ride and was beaten a length. The following year Why Not was again ridden by Mr. Cunningham but fell. Remounted he finished fifth. Then he changed stables and was third in 1893 (ridden by Arthur Nightingall), and in 1894, with the same jockey up, won the National by a length carrying top weight, 11st 13lbs. In 1888 Mr. Nevett cared for Matin Bell, also trained by Harry Hall, and winner that year of the Northumberland Plate. She was ridden by Seth Chandley and owned by Charles Perkins, who had been responsible six years earlier for having Newcastle Races moved from the bad course on the Town Moor to the present track at Gosforth Park.

Mr. Nevett added "exactly fifty years after I took Matin Bell to win the Northumberland Plate, my son rode the winner of the race on Union Jack."

Willie had not nearly the same number of mounts as Sir Gordon or the opportunity to pick and choose his rides as had the champion jockey, but his average was always much better than that of Richards. In some characteristics the two jockeys were alike. Success never turned the head of either, or destroyed their modesty and both were bright and cheery under all circumstances. In other respects they were totally dissimilar. For instance, the Richards family had no sort of connection with horses or riding, before Sir Gordon became a jockey.

Willie Nevett was apprenticed to Dobson Peacock and finished his apprenticeship in 1930. Willie was of course champion jockey of the north for 25 years, and was successful in 2,065 races. In 1953 he rode 100 winners in one season for the eighth time and his best year was 1947 when he won 136 events. For many years he was runner-up in the championship to Sir Gordon. There is a story — probably apocryphal — that when Willie first rode at Newmarket he overheard Gordon ask "who is this Northern jockey MacNevett?" Vowed Willie: "I'll MacNevett him" — and went out to ride three winners. Willie rode for three generations of the Peacock family.

The Newmarket story is completely out of character for Sir Gordon. Both the British and the Northern champions preferred to be seen and not heard — and both were tremendously lucky to be natural lightweights. A young jockey the other day tried his weight on arriving at a North country course. He had had no breakfast, had spent an hour or more in a Turkish bath, and found he was lighter than he expected. He therefore felt justified in having a drink and sucking an orange. To his astonishment he was told when weighing out for the race for which he had been wasting, that he was 2lb overweight. He took off his vest, got a lighter saddle, and drew the correct weight. He could not understand how a drink and the juice of an orange had put on more than 2lb to his weight. On several occasions when I was acting as clerk-of-scales, leading jockeys who came to weigh out a pound overweight were most anxious that this should not go on the number-board and pleaded with me "Can't you pass me as I am? There's so little in it." Usually we compromised, a scarf and wither pad being discarded. I remember on one of the first occasions I acted as clerk-of-scales telling one or two well-known jockeys to get a lighter saddle. One of the valets – himself an ex-jockey – came to remonstrate with me. He said: "Don't weight them out as though they were gold. There's always a couple of pounds to play with." It is almost unbelievable how a jockey who has been wasting will put on weight out of all proportion to what he consumes if he yields to the craving to quench his thirst.

Jim Fagan once told me that wasting hard and fasting to ride at York, he succeeded in getting off nearly 4lb. In the paddock he found he could not resist buying a small pear from a fruit stall. On gong to the scale he found he had put on over 1lb. George Johnson, who, after his jockey days was long head man for Fred Bates at Middleham, was engaged to ride Bersaglier in the Ascot Stakes. Despite baths, physic and fasting he told the trainer he would have to ride 2lb overweight. Bates would not agree, and said he would find another jockey. Off went the hungry Johns for a sandwich. A substitute jockey could not be found, so Bates chased round for Johnson and told him to declare the 2lb overweight. On getting into the scale the jockey was now more than 4lb too heavy, so another jockey was given the ride and was just beaten.

Many times I have heard Bob Armstrong tell the story of undoing an exhausting 36 mile weight-reducing walk by having a glass of lemonade. In his Penrith days he put on an overcoat on a hot afternoon and tramped the 18 miles into Carlisle. There he had a glass of mineral water before he walked back. On arriving at Penrith he found he was more than 2lb heavier than when he had set off.

The most remarkable instance of weight reduction within my knowledge was that of Robert Antail Jones at Newmarket in 1940. To ride Real Estate he reduced his weight from 9st 6½lb to 8st 8lb in 24 hours. He was rewarded by winning at 10-1. I well remember the case of Joe Marshall, who was born at Burley-in-Wharfedale, but moved to Edinburgh as a child. He won the 1929 Derby on Trigo and then crossed to France to ride. Returning after a couple of seasons he went to Middleham to ride for Bob Armstrong, but he put on weight and was continually wasting. At Hamilton Park in August 1932 he was engaged to ride Caress at 8st 2lb. A couple of hours before racing he put on a sweater and ran round the course at least once. He then lay in the jockeys' room with perspiration rolling off him. He weighed out correctly, but feeling faint and parched he got one of the jockeys' valets to bring him half a bottle of champagne. I saw this carried through the weighing-room in an innocent looking teapot. Caress was favourite and there was a tremendous finish in which Blue Finch, ridden by Willie Christie, won by a neck. When Marshall came to scale to weigh in as second he was more than 2lb heavier than when he was weighed out, so Caress was disqualified. There was a stewards' enquiry at which Joe frankly owned up about the thirst and the fizz.

Other instances could be quoted of a morsel of food, or a drink, having added pounds to the weight of a wasting jockey. There have been other reasons why jockeys presenting themselves at scales have been much heavier or lighter than when they weighed out. I remember a mystery of this sort being solved at Ripon when it was found that Percy Botterill had picked up a wrong saddle from the rail in the weighing-room and put it on to a horse he trained. The horse won but was disqualified because his jockey could not draw the weight.

The Racing Calendar for 1842 chronicles a remarkable "wrong weight" case. In a two-year-old race at Newmarket (colts 8st 7lb, fillies 8st 4lb) a filly named Barmaid beat the colt Pickpocket by a head. The Calendar adds this note to the official return: "Pickpocket was frightened by the rustling of the silk jacket, in consequence of which his rider put on a coat which made his weight 8st 9½lb."

Those who live to be 90 find, as I do, that they have a lot of acquaintances on the Turf but few friends. We have outlived our generation. One by one those with whom we were really intimate, those before whom we could think aloud — and knew there would be a sympathetic hearing — have nearly all preceded us into the great unknown. A few still remain who are regularly seen racing. A few more are as interested as ever but enjoy their racing televised. One of these is ex-jockey Jack Anderson. I was delighted to hear from him after he was roped in to represent jockeys at the Blaydon Races centenary celebrations on Tyneside. He was also the subject of a television interview, and has sent me a photo of himself and others taking part in the Blaydon Races festival. Jack was one of two Hull brothers who became jockeys. George, the elder, served his time with William Elsey at Baumber and then rode for some time in Austria. On returning to this country he started as a trainer at Beverley. Latterly he had an hotel at Hornsea, where he died in 1952.

Jack, was apprenticed to Melton Vasey, and rode his first winner at Catterick in 1906. I remember Melton then telling me that he had never known a lad who made such a study of horses' temperaments. "He can get more out of a rogue, or sluggish horse by kidding to it than other jockeys can by knocking them about," added Melton. Of all the winners he rode Jack Anderson said none gave him such a thrill as that on Lester Reiff owned and trained by ex-jockey Yorky Priestman.

This was in September 1909 at Hull when Jack achieved his ambition to ride a winner at his birthplace. He was just in time to do this because the revival of flat racing on Hedon course was short-lived and there was no more racing there after 1909. After the First World War Sir Loftus Bates and I went to look at the course and buildings to see if another revival was worth trying but decided against it. Jack Anderson's last winner was Gracious Son at Carlisle in 1947. He was then assisting Graham Mather — who trained the winner — at Richmond.

It is always good at Hexham and Newcastle meetings to see John Straker — a descendent of the Strakers in the Confederacy — taking such an interest in everything, and wonderfully bright and cheerful in his wheelchair. Everyone admires his spirit and courage. Despite a spinal injury in 1961 at Perth races depriving him of one of the greatest joys in his life — the feel of a good horse underneath him — he continues his interest in running his farm, his horses in training and his stud, all within a few miles of Hexham course. He is one of a select band in the North who, though incapacitated through riding accidents, refuse to be defeated and continue to enjoy racing.

It is remarkable how many sportsmen and sportswomen have recovered from what are usually fatal accidents — a broken neck or fractured spine. I have already mentioned Col. Milvain, who went on hunting hounds for thirty years after breaking his neck. Maud Cheape, broke her neck riding in a point-to-point and made a wonderful recovery. So did Charles Mulholland, who had a similar accident when riding at Rothbury in 1927. He later trained at Carlisle and rode in the show ring and went fox hunting. Yet another, who rode as well as ever after breaking his neck, was Harry Marshall. He was South Durham huntsman during the Mastership of Lord Southampton when it happened in 1931. He married a sister of the well-known owner and Cambridgeshire MFH, Douglas Crossman. He had horses with Bobby Renton and Walter Easterby and then himself trained for some years between

Bedale and Middleham. Probably as a thank-offering, he made his home a convalescing place for jockeys when they left hospital after being injured when riding. Unfortunately he got the worst of his tilts at the ring and could not come racing during the latter years of his life. He died in Scotland in 1961 at the age of 80.

Of course the most historic case of a jockey breaking his neck and not only recovering but also riding in the Grand National the following year, was that of Lord Minto, who – using his Eton nick-name – rode as "Mr. Rolly." He was for years, one of the leading amateurs. When riding Zero in the 1878 Grand National "Mr. Rolly" fractured his neck. He was told by the eminent surgeon, Sir James Paget, that he would never ride again. Later Sir James said he was a marvel to be alive, and that his skeleton would be of great interest to the College of Surgeons. I remember being thrilled and honoured by an invitation to dine with Lord Minto at Hawick after Kelso races in 1910. I wish tape-recorders had been invented then, for his reminiscences and opinions on Turf matters were well worth preserving. He died at Minto House, Hawick, on March 1 1914, after being Governor-General of Canada and Viceroy of India.

Lionel Vick is yet another of the steeplechase jockeys who have been able to lead useful lives after experiencing a fractured vertebrae. He had a bad fall at Sedgefield in 1951 and though now confined to a wheelchair is a successful chartered accountant. He gives a lot of his spare time helping the Stoke Mandeville Hospital, at which he spent many months. Poor Lionel! What a good jockey he was, and what a bright future was cut short by cruel fate! I sometimes hear from him and always he recalls the way I used to chaff him, and then send him off happy with a luncheon ticket. He was a nice lightweight, so able to enjoy a hearty meal before racing, when some other jockeys who had probably spent the morning in a Turkish bath, were not able to have a bite. When his accident happened he was attached to

Charlie Hall's Tadcaster stable. He rode his first winner when he was 15 for Bob Gore at Plumpton but had been riding to hounds in Surrey — where his father trained — long before that. Although a Southerner, Lionel, like many others, preferred northern racing where he said he found quite a different and far more sporting atmosphere. Wetherby was his favourite course. Personally I consider it about the best National Hunt course in the country, especially since the new hurdle track was laid down and first used at the final 1962 meeting.

Just before that season, Major and Mrs. W. T. Lipscomb celebrated their golden wedding. The Major had some of his famed vintage port decanted for the celebrations at the Manor House, Thorp Arch, as well as a case of champagne sent him by sporting friends. He has for years provided the port from his cellar for the Boxing Day meeting at Wetherby, and I have never failed to join the stewards when the decanters have been going round. Indeed, I once heard my old friend Col. "Squeak" Thompson say, "No vintage port — no stewards!" For over thirty years Major Lipscomb was clerk of the course at Wetherby and at over 80 must have been the oldest one in the country. He was born at Heath, near Wakefield in 1881. He was for 50 years agent for the Bramham estate, and in addition had the management of some famous Yorkshire grouse moors. For a quarter of a century he was honorary secretary of the Bramham Moor Hunt. He went well to hounds and was, in his day, one of the best game shots in the North. The Wetherby meeting justifies the title "the Cheltenham of the North" and, in recent years, has been the main concern of the Major's life. I officiated there until my retirement in 1961, when his son, Mr. V. Lipscomb succeeded me.

Of jockeys, sufficient stories could be told to fill a book. John Osborne told me once he received so many instructions from an owner as to how he was to ride that he said on his unvictorious return, "The course couldn't be found long enough to carry out all the orders given." John once replied to another owner who blamed him for not "coming on" according to instructions: "I couldn't come on without the horse!" At Haydock Park – then known as Newton – "Speedy" Payne was hauled up before the Stewards – a particularly swell lot on that occasion. Payne was asked to explain his riding and addressed the Stewards: "My Lords, dukes, admirals, colonels and gentlemen: When I rides and wins they says I rides foul. When I rides and loses they says I pulls. I have a wife at home, some money in the bank and I doesn't care a damn what you does with me!" The stewards were so amused that they let Speedy go without so much as a caution.

At Hexham, George Gunter was called before the stewards for apparently coming in with a great rush at the finish when too late to win after having allowed his horse to go to pieces. The secret of the matter was that he was riding with a broken stirrup leather and could manage very well when he came to the flat, however, he briefly replied to questions: "Gentlemen, I am not a circus performer!"

Catterick paddock was once nearly the scene of a duel when the great Sir Tatton Sykes beat George Baker in an amateur riders' race. Sir Tatton waved his whip to the ladies on the stand as he passed the judges' box first and Baker by some means translated this into an insult – a public crowing over his own defeat. The duel didn't take place, but when Sir Tatton was at a sheep sale a short time afterwards Baker bid up some rams the Sledmore baronet wanted to buy to hundreds of pounds.

It was in the Catterick paddock too, that Jim Snowden, one of the best jockeys who ever threw a leg over a horse, came out of the weighing-room rather more drunk than usual. He asked to have his mount pointed and then said, "Nay! Nay! take them blinkers off him; a blinnd hoss and a blinnd jockey'll nivver deea." William I'Anson always said that Jim Snowden was the best jockey he ever saw no matter whether he was drunk or sober. On one occasion after a drinking bout Snowden arrived at Chester, at which meeting he had – or should have had –

many mounts. He remarked to the landlord that the town seemed very quiet for racetime. "Race-time!" came the reply "why, Jim, you're a week over late! The races were last week." Snowden got his first mount in a peculiar manner. He was born at Pocklington and when a tiny lad often rode at little country flapping meetings. He shaped so well and enjoyed the game so much he decided he would become a jockey so set off to Doncaster Leger meeting. The man at the gate wouldn't let him in, so Jim, not to be beaten, went on to the course and climbed the railings into the paddock. Someone who had seen him riding at "flaps" and village feast races got him a mount. His dash and style caught the eye of some Northern trainers who gave him plenty of riding so that he soon made his name.

Lance Barker, in addition to farming Mill Vale, near Broughton, Stokesley, running a meat trade business, and acting as a very skilful amateur vet, ran a lot of horses in the early part of this century, particularly under National Hunt rules. He used to ride well and won many races on horses trained by his father at Redcar. One of Lance's first winners was Crawley Daisy, bred by the father of the successful Bishop Auckland trainer, Arthur Stephenson. When riding at Sedgefield in 1928 Lance had a bad fall which resulted in total loss of sight. Never once did I hear him express any self pity, or complain about this hard luck. A strange thing about Lance was that as soon as any old friends spoke to him he immediately identified them and cheerily greeted them by their name. Even after he had lost his sight Lance popped horses he had for sale over fences to show their abilities to prospective customers. He had an odd day with hounds and occasionally rode exercise on Redcar sands on some of his brother's team. Ever since that unlucky day at Sedgefield he showed the true sportsman's courage and refusal to admit defeat. There was once a jockey in Scotland who went on riding in races after he had become blind. His name was McGilvray and the grandfather of the Malton trainer Billy Binnie, was among those who put him up. On the other hand, Jimmy Thompson thought it unfair to other jockeys to continue riding in races after he lost the sight of one eye due to a stone being thrown up and hitting him in a race at Newcastle, which was not far from where he was born.

Harry Edwards, one of the leading jockeys of the 19th century was also blind in one eye. A contemporary writer describes him as "perhaps the most accomplished finisher of a race, and one of the finest horsemen ever seen." After his high assessment the same authority (Sylvanus) adds that John Scott the famous Malton trainer had to get rid of Edwards when he "stopped" a horse that the stable had backed heavily. "Harry would rather 'nobble' for a pony than get a hundred pounds by fair means," commented Scott, who trained 41 classic winners. Edwards ruined his career and went to Nantes where he trained, rode, trained and nobbled in a small way.

I remember a number of blind owners of racehorses. Among them John Hill, a Middlesbrough iron merchant, who lived at Saltburn until he moved to Kingston, where he died in 1921. He had horses with William I'Anson, the best of them being Mintagon. I recall his son advising me some weeks beforehand to back Mintagon, then at a long price for the 1906 Ebor Handicap. I was with William I'Anson on the stand at York when Mintagon was just beaten for the Ebor and together we read the race for Mr. Hill. At the subsequent Gimcrack Dinner — which I attended longer than any living man — Mr. Hill was a guest. He had a room engaged for refreshments after the dinner, and amongst those invited to enjoy his hospitality was John Corlett, editor and proprietor of the now defunct *Pink 'Un* to which I contributed. The following week Corlett wrote: "After the Gimcrack dinner a few adjourned to the room of Mr. Hill, the owner of Mintagon, and the conversation ran on the Ebor and Cesarewitch. When a man is blind, or loses any of the senses, the others become more acute, and so it is with Mr. Hill. He looks and talks as though he had seen everything. It was startling to hear him say, apropos of Maher's fine riding on Golden Measure that cost Mintagon the Ebor Handicap: 'Most people thought he had not got up, but I could see that

PLATE 11
The author with Captain Riley Lord in the Redcar Parade ring. Edward Hides' mount obviously impresses.

PLATE 12
Harry Lane receives the Catterick Grand National Trial Trophy from the author in 1962, having been successful with Jolly Jester.

PLATE 13
One of the last photographs taken of the author shows him in his library at Low House in 1975. He died the following January.

he had.' He gathered this merely from what he heard of the race."

When Mintagon won the 1906 Cesarewitch, Mr. Hill said to I'Anson: "I could see for myself how easily he won." Like many others connected with Cleveland iron trade Mr. Hill fell on evil days and sold his horses to James Byrne, who also lived at Saltburn and was in the coal trade at Middlesbrough. Byrne, who died in 1915, leaving over £42,000, owned Mercutio, who ran well in the Two Thousand Guineas and in the Stewards' Cup. Mercutio was probably a better horse than his performances indicated. Mr. Byrne had his horses at Newmarket with an Australian named Edwin Couch but eventually tired of him, and Couch committed suicide at Torquay on hearing that Mercutio had won the 1911 Lincolnshire Handicap. By that time Mercutio had passed into the hands of the Nottingham bookmaker Charlie Hibbert who was a fearless better and won a lot of money at Lincoln over this hitherto disappointing horse. There was a big field and Mercutio (100-12) was second favourite. Jack Barnato Joel fancied his Spanish Prince and had a bet of £50,000 to £5,000 with Hibbert, who stood the lot and straightway went and invested the £5,000 on his own horse.

Hibbert, who died in 1915, left over £100,000. I remember once when he had a horse running someone saying to him "You've won it there, Charlie," to which Hibbert replied "A lot of horses have won it there! When my money's down I want 'em to win here" — pointing to the winning post. Stanley Ford, long a turf judge and clerk of course at several meetings, married one of Hibbert's daughters.

I remember too, Fred Holland, whose father hunted the Bedale Hounds, coming racing after he had lost his sight through the branch of a tree swishing across his face as he jumped a fence. He was making a name for himself as huntsman for A. Paget Steavenson. I had many chats with Fred after he had lost his sight. He retired to Masham and used to be brought to Thirsk and Catterick meetings to meet old friends. There has always been a strong bond between the racing and hunting world.

I have known several owners who could not stand the excitement of watching their horses run. One was the late John Hamer, the Bolton brewer, who used to pace up and down behind the stands at race meetings when he had a fancied runner. He was a very wealthy man but his final days were marred by the hallucination that he was a pauper. Another brewer with whom I was long friendly was the old Etonian W. Riley-Smith of Tadcaster. Dobson Peacock trained for him for many years and lots of happy days I had with Riley-Smith both at Middleham and his home Toulston, near Tadcaster. His daughter-in-law is keeping the Turf flag flying. Mrs. Douglas Riley-Smith has horses with Dick Peacock at Middleham. His father and grandfather both trained for Riley-Smith one of whose best horses was Scottish Archer, which Matt Peacock bought for him out of a seller at Manchester. He was trained and ridden by Frank Brown — an old friend of Riley-Smith's who had strict instructions to buy him in. Matt Peacock knew nothing about this, and later Frank Brown told the new owner of Scottish Archer that he had got into hot water for allowing him to go. Scottish Archer won 11 races for Riley-Smith, who once rode him himself in a "bumper's" event at Catterick. I remember the day well when the heavyweight Tadcaster brewer came to scale. In his privately printed *Memories* — he sent me a copy inscribed "Hush Hush!" shortly before his death in 1954 and some of the stories are very private — there is an amusing description of his efforts to reduce weight: "The early martyrs were supposed to go through great privations but they were child's play to what I went through. I was dropped at York twice a week and walked home to Tadcaster, this giving me varicose veins. About three times a week for six weeks I got into the mash tub at the brewery, and there got a tremendous sweat up. My meals were the sort Gandhi would have had when he had jaundice. I gave up wine, women, and never bothered to sing. This lasted till the great day. When I went into the weighing-room to change, trainers came in, pointed to my stomach, and went into fits of laughter. When I got into the scale feeling like a new born babe, I weighed 12st 12lb, and was supposed to carry 12st 2lb. At the starting-post Gerald Armstrong introduced me to someone who was contesting in the same great race. I did not know whether to shake hands with him or take my cap off."

Another old-timer from who I was always glad to hear was Mrs. E. Plummer, whom I have known all my life. She lived at Carlton Husthwaite, near Thirsk. Mrs. Plummer has a rich sporting background. She bred bloodstock for years and sold Friar's Daughter (dam of Bahram) to the Aga Khan. I remember well when lunching with Fred Fox at Carlisle Races, he told me that Bahram was the greatest horse he had ever ridden or seen — "a perfect gentleman, with the manners of a ladies' hack." Bahram, of course, was never beaten, among his triumphs were the Derby and St. Leger. He was foaled in 1932. Mrs. Plummer's father, William Sanderson, trained at Hambelton for some years before going to Malton. His son Walter, was private trainer to Mr. Larnach who won the 1898 Derby with Jeddah. Mrs. Plummer's husband was one of a Thormanby, near Thirsk, family, long connected with the Turf as breeders and owners. The horse which gained most fame for their stud was Thormanby, which won the 1860 Derby for James Merry. He cleared £80,000 in bets over the race but his present to Harry Custance, the successful jockey, was £100 only.

CHAPTER NINE

TRICKS OF THE TRADE

When I was young there were much stranger things done on the Turf than could be accomplished these days. Stewards are much more vigilant and knowledgeable. In 1908 I remember a Malton owner running a horse at Thirsk in a race which looked a gift for him. He was made favourite, but the owner backed the ultimate winner. He had a jockey who "was paid and did as he was told." His instructions were to get well away, make the running, and then pull up and dismount a couple of furlongs from home. At the spot indicated the horse pulled up, the jockey dismounted, and the owner, who was standing conveniently near, rushed on to the course. Covered by the jockey he produced from a warm inside pocket a bottle, and with his handkerchief smeared the horse's nostrils with the blood he had that morning collected from a Malton slaughterhouse. Together jockey and owner led the horse back to the paddock with blood trickling from its nostrils and the gory handkerchief much displayed. It was obvious for everyone to THINK that this was a bad case of blood-vessel breaking. The following week the same horse ran at another Yorkshire meeting but no one except the owner dare take the long odds offered. He won and there was no summons to the stewards room afterwards. A broken blood-vessel may, of course, mean nothing to the future success of a horse. Countless cases might be cited in proof of this. One which helped to make turf history, was that of the 1867 Derby winner Hermit. Ten days before the Derby, Mr. (later Viscount) Chaplin's horse broke a blood vessel and Lady Londonderry (Lord Chaplin's daughter), who knew all the circumstances, recorded the details of the winding-up gallop prior to Epsom: "For a mile in the gallop Hermit was pulling Custance out of the saddle, then Hermit coughed, blood poured from his nostrils, and he all but collapsed in his stride. His Derby chance was apparently extinct. It was found at Newmarket that his case was not so serious as at first thought. He resumed work and on the Saturday before Epsom, Capt. Machell gave him canters of a mile each the reverse way to the Rowley Mile. In these he did well."

But the news of the broken blood-vessel was public property, and no one except Hermit's owner and the friends who took his advice, would back the horse. In consequence his starting price was 100 to 15. Mr. Chaplin won a huge stake apart from the heavy wager he had with the ill-fated young Marquis of Hastings, who lost over £120,000 over the race. Hermit never again broke a blood vessel and at stud sired five classic winners — Thebais, Shotover, St. Marguerite, St. Blaise and Lonely.

Tommy Courtney had a whole boxful of Turf tricks. As I have mentioned he used to buy a lot of horses to send abroad mainly to run on the Continent. He had a standing order from Belgium for animals which had run 1, 2 or 3 in this country. One bought for export he felt sure could win a selling race before he shipped it. Those were days when assumed names were allowed and under a *nom-de-course* he entered the filly for a seller at Stockton. He wanted neither to lose her nor to have to pay through the nose to buy her back at the auction when she had won. He ran her in bandages and before the auctioneer began the sale, he got the lad in charge to remove the bandages, ran his hand down both fore-legs, and holding up both hands in feigned horror at her tendons, stood back sniggering. Everyone knew Tommy and what a good judge he was, so there was no bid, and to Courtney's relief the auctioneer said: "Take her away!"

In my time there have been many cases of horses running under wrong names. Most of them were due to accidental confusion, and were at once reported to the Jockey Club by owner or trainer when the discovery was made. In one or two instances this was not until the incorrectly described animal had won a race or two and there have, of course, been a number of fraudulent substitutions. Those which have been detected have rocked the Turf as nine days' wonders. The one I best remember was in the two-year-old Maiden Faceby Plate at Stockton on October 25, 1919. The villainy did not come to light for some time afterwards when it was proved that the winner — 5-2 favourite Coat of Mail — was actually the three year-old Jaz. The real Coat of Mail was a two-year-old bay which had never run but the other colt, Jaz (a brown), had had several outings and had run second at Stockton in the Middlesbrough Welter Handicap in August, 1919. A few days later he was again second, this time at Gatwick. He was then sold by Sir Hedworth Meux — one of the Lambton family. There was quite a party concerned in this Stockton substitution ramp, the main organiser being the well-known Peter Christian ("Ringer") Barris who went to gaol. Walter Hosking, William Hy Collins and Horace Samuel Berg were warned off.

I remember several cases of quite unintentional substitution of horses owing to mistaken identity. In 1927 Dobson Peacock had Faiza, a three-year-old and Ayot a four-year-old sent by their lady owner and breeder to train at Middleham. There was confusion on arrival and the filly assumed to be Faiza was nominated for three-year-old events. After being bought by Adam Boazman an old patron of Peacock's she won three races in succession. Later, Ayot was sent back to her owner who at once saw that it was Faiza which had arrived. Faiza had been running as Ayot and vice versa.

Seven years later there was a similar "mix-up" at Walter Pollock's Malton stable. Horace Brueton an owner, breeder and bookmaker, sent him three yearlings. Two of them were bay geldings named Blytheway and Old Jack. Their identity was mistaken by Pollock and each ran in the name of the other for two seasons before the error was discovered and reported. As neither of them had won a race it didn't matter much. It was different in the historic case of Mortaigne and D'Orsay, for both won races when running in each other's name. Their breeder, R. H. Harrison, whose stud was then near Ripon, eventually called attention to the quite innocent mistake.

How easy it was for experts to substitute horses is abundantly proved by the fact that there are several well-authenticated cases of animals being stolen, trimmed up and markings stained, then sold to their erstwhile owners at horse fairs. Hogging the mane, "cropping" the ears — a now obsolete practice — cutting the horses' tail and painting out white markings on the face or legs, so alters the appearance of horses that in days when supervision was less strict, many unscrupulous owners succeeded in substituting one animal for another. There are, however, many men who have a wonderful memory for horses. Once they have really closely examined an animal they never seem to forget it. So was it that in the long run these rogues of the Turf were found out and "warned off."

In recent years there have been one or two attempts — but there is little of this "disguising" horses nowadays either at training quarters or on the racecourse. It has been proved beyond all doubt that to be successful as a scoundrel on the Turf a man must either work single-handed or must have accomplices who are deaf, dumb, unable to write and without any memory. Failing this one or the other knowing the secret invariably imagines he has not got sufficient good red gold for holding his tongue and lets the cat out of the bag.

William I'Anson once told me he arranged to disguise some horses to be tried on York racecourse, so that no tout would be able to tell what animals were galloped, let alone which had won. He took the animals to the wood on the far side of Knavesmire and, with a bucket of Fuller's-earth and paint he gave some of them white legs and blazes right down their faces, and painted out the natural white legs of others. J. B. Cookson, partner with Charlie Perkins in so many good horses, and long Master of the Morpeth Hunt, was sent to the finishing point to act as judge and when the horses he had seen during the process of their painting, passed him, he hadn't the remotest idea which was which or what had won, though he had a share in all the animals. Jockeys had been engaged to ride in the trial and they had to be consulted as to which had won and what were the placings of the others.

This system of disguising horses was frequently resorted to by trainers who wished to hoodwink the touts. They were perfectly justified in such action. This enabled their employers to get their money on before someone else had taken the cream off the market on hearing from their hired "watcher" at training quarters how certain animals had gone in a stripped gallop. It was when horses were brought to race-meetings so disguised that they might, and often did, pass for some other animals, that real villainy entered into the matter.

In the earliest days of racing it was a rule that all owners produced the horses at the time of their entry so that they might be seen and recognised and their ages proved by the markings on their teeth. However necessary this was at the time it would be quite impossible in these days. Then racing was to a great extent local. South country horses rarely came north and those from the north seldom competed with the southern brigade. Indeed when the southerners began to come to Doncaster to try their luck in the St Leger, there was tremendous feeling against them and once or twice the race was packed with all sorts of impossible animals which went to the post with no other object than the hamper and shut in the "foreigners" as they were called.

Even the inspection at the time of entry did not prevent one horse from being sent to take the place of another on many occasions. This was particularly the case in races for half-breds which were once so popular. The conditions were that the animals were not to be pure thoroughbreds and that they were not to have been at a training stable. Frequently those who wanted to win big sums from the ring, entered a three-parts bred hunter but on the day of the race, brought a thoroughbred, possibly by the same sire and very like the animal entered.

William Day, the famous trainer, used to tell a story of substitution at Northampton. E. Jones, who trained near Marlborough, had a three-year-old colt by Melbourne, named Brocket, and also a two-year-old filly by Bay Middleton, named Ruby. The latter was engaged to run at Northampton in a two-year-old race and, without the knowledge of his owner (Mr. B. Way) Brocket was also taken to the meeting though not a runner. Ruby was notoriously a hot, nervous runaway youngster so that the stewards' permission was easily obtained for her to be led to the post and mounted there so missing the usual parade in front of the stands and in the paddock. But it was Brocket which was walked down to the paddock covered up with sheets and with a hood on. Bartholomew, who had previously ridden Brocket a winner, ought to have known – perhaps he did! – that it was the colt and not the filly he was mounting. Of course the three-year-old colt won in a common canter. As soon as he had passed the post, he was covered up with sheets again and led away to one of the closed boxes on the course and soon left for home. The bookies paid out and it was not for some time that the whole story became known. This strikes one as a particularly daring bit of deceit – not merely to run a three-year-old for a two-year-old but to represent a filly by a colt.

The most famous case of substitution in the history of the Turf was that of Running Rein in the 1844 Derby. It was not Running Rein which won the great Epsom classic but a four-year-old horse called Maccabaeus. Running Rein had been spirited away by his owner, Goodman Levy – known on the Turf as Goodman – and another of his horses, the year older Maccabaeus, was sent to take his place at the training quarters. The real Running Rein was hidden away at Finchley and it was given out that Maccabaeus was dead. But the dead animal, under the name of Running Rein, won a two-year-old race at Newmarket and rumour was rife at once. The Duke of Rutland – who had heard the story – claimed the stake on the grounds that the winner was a three-year-old. Goodman was able to call evidence which satisfied the stewards that the horse was Running Rein and a two-year-old. A youth from Malton, who had assisted at the foaling of the real Running Rein, convinced them. Goodman, thinking that no one would have the temerity to raise the question again, sent Maccabaeus to Epsom to take the place of the real Running Rein in the following year's Derby. Objections were lodged before the race and it was intimated to Goodman that if the horse won, the stakes would be withheld for full enquiries. Nevertheless Goodman ran Running Rein — alias Maccabaeus — and won. Then Lord George Bentinck took the matter up and eventually Goodman was charged and taken to court. There it was abundantly proved that there had been a wilful and flagrant fraud, and Lord George was able to produce a London hairdresser named Rossi, from whom Goodman had purchased hair-dye to disguise Maccabaeus. In his summing up Baron Alderson, who tried the case, said: "The evidence has produced great regret and disgust to my mind. It has disclosed a horrible fraud, and has shown noblemen and gentlemen of rank associating with and betting with men of low status and infinitely below them in society. In so doing they have found themselves cheated and made the dupes of the grossest frauds. They may depend upon it that this will always be so when gentlemen associate with blackguards."

The famous old-time trainer, John Kent — who had charge of Lord George Bentinck's horses — points out another remarkable fact in connection with Running Rein's Derby. Two other horses started for the race were four-year-olds and one of them broke the leg of the other going round Tattenham Corner.

A final story regarding disguise. This occurred a few years ago at Ripon when Bob Robson had Marsden Rock running and before taking him into the paddock, had him splashed with mud and his hair rubbed up the wrong way till he looked "a dog horse." Poor old J. A. Whipp was making a book in those days and on seeing Marsden Rock he chaffed "Bob" about bringing such a brute. Giving a £10 note to a friend, Robson said: "Go and stand by Whipp and when he shouts '10 to 1 Marsden Rock' pop that into his hand." This was done and when "the brute" had won comfortably – Robson had backed him well with other layers – he had the laugh over his old friend who had said such hard things about his "coal-cart horse" and "brute." Yet there were few men more astute than Whipp at most times!

When there was less vigilance on the part of Stewards, the story was generally believed that Bob Adams had won a 1901 Sedgefield race – by travelling only half the distance. Bob always denied the accusation, but was said to have taken full advantage of a foggy afternoon and hidden behind a haystack during the first circuit of a steeplechase. The haystack was on the far side of the course, and the tale was that Bob remained hidden until the horses approached for the final lap. Then he jumped off in front and won easily.

At country meetings about the turn of the century it was not uncommon for jockeys who found that they were going to win on un-backed horses, to slip out of the saddle to the ground. Sometimes they first disengaged and dropped a stirrup-leather and iron. I remember Bob Harper, who was born in 1862 and rode successfully for many years, telling me that he had done this falling act so often that he had become quite a circus performer and was never any the worse. Of course, it is a very different matter falling off by design to meeting the ground without warning when going racing pace. Bob Harper began as a boy riding at flapping meetings when there were many of them in the North. Then he was for years with George Menzies, who trained at Coxhoe in County Durham. From him he went to George Gunter, at Wetherby, and was his head man for over 30 years. Riding Marcolica at Wetherby in 1912, Bob made a record jump. The horse took off 15 feet before a hurdle, landed 27 feet over it and then slithered 18 feet before falling and pushing Bob another 20 feet along the ground. Latterly he acted as starter at a number of Northern National Hunt meetings. He was up to every dodge in the racing game, and on one occasion when he was starter at Wetherby I remember him causing a good deal of amusement to some distinguished amateur riders. They had mounts in a big field for a hurdle race and Harper, after a good deal of trouble at the post, lost his patience and called out: "Will those of you who are *trying* line up and I'll get YOU off." There was another amusing incident in which Bob was main actor. It was at Haydock Park in 1912. He had brought a good horse of Gunter's and I also had a runner. We both went to the racecourse stables before breakfast to see the horses, and on the way back a man stopped Bob and asked him if Holly Lodge was fancied later in the day. Without a word, Bob took an old envelope from his pocket, produced a pencil, then said: "I tell you — that's I." He wrote I on the envelope. "You tell somebody else — that's II." Then (adding a third I), he said: "He tells somebody else — how many's that?" "Three" replied the information hunter. "No!" retorted Bob, "It's one hundred and eleven, so good morning!" Bob who I saw a lot of in his palmy days, was a good and bold horseman, with a dry sense of humour. He knew every move on the board, was as straight as could be and as honest as the day with those who played the game, but quite prepared to pay the foul riders and "clever brigade" back in their own coin.

I well remember a North country trainer telling me in 1912 that he knew a race was a certainty for one of his horses — but for one 'chaser which was sure to win if it ran. In those days there was little racecourse stabling provided, so trainers had to get their horses into such stalls and boxes as they could find in inn-yards. The trainer who related the story to me had a runner in the same yard as the horse he knew would beat him. He devised a plan to prevent this without doing the feared rival any lasting harm. He would "nobble" it, but not after the manner of those who "got at" horses in the old days and stopped at no cruelty to achieve their ends — poison, maiming, and in one case, cutting out the tongue of a heavily backed horse. The trainer plied the lad in charge of the rival horse with drink until the boy had to be put to bed. After seeing him fast asleep the trainer took the stable-key from the lad's pocket, went into his horse's box, and gave the "certainty" a physic-ball, fully expecting that it would make it impossible for the horse to run the following day. To the surprise of the doper, however, the horse turned up on the course. There was no doubt about the ball having worked. The horse's hocks bore evidence of this. But he ran and won despite the "doctoring".

Some of us who have long been very closely associated with the Turf are very tired of dope discussions and nobbling sensations. The general public wallow in both and have spoon-fed sensational syrup – much of it exaggerated or pure mythical imagination, all of it unwise – continually fed to them by the lay Press. It is more because of the suspicion aroused by all this, than established fact, that all the "security" precautions have been instituted. They may give confidence to the fearful but they have given a totally wrong impression as to the morals of the Turf. I doubt the existence of bands of villains constantly scheming and ready to carry out all manner of diabolical plots to stop horses winning races, or to so stimulate sluggish or moderate animals that they will win events in which they apparently have no chance.

CHAPTER TEN

LOOKING BACK – AND FORWARDS

I am fascinated by the recent moves to form a union for stable lads, and by the argument provoked. This was nothing compared with the vituperation I received when I tried to form an association to protect stable boys in 1910 – yes, more than 65 years ago. The union I proposed was to be an agency for supplying trainers with suitable lads of proved character. Possibly later a school for riding would have been formed and maintained. The union would also have served to protect the interests of lads in stables and to improve their conditions and would have acted between lads and trainers in case of dispute. Also the agency would have found suitable situations for those who had spent the best part of their lives in racing stables, but who, because of increased weight, injury or redundancy had to leave stables.

A percentage of about one in a hundred of the boys who enter racing stables with the expectation of becoming jockeys and riding their way to fame and fortune ever reach the bottom step to that pinnacle. Many of them never have the opportunity of even riding on a racecourse. Some of these fit naturally into the Turf sphere and live their lives happily as stable staff. Others find that they are unsuited to this routine and quit racing bitter with disappointment. So at a critical time in their lives and unqualified for any employment except with horses, they are thrown out with little chance. My hope was to protect those in the industry and those who had to leave. Opposition from the Jockey Club and Bob Sievier's *The Winning Post* spelled death for my aims.

The Winning Post saw my efforts as a disaster to the sport, and Siever's fury and scorn made modern-day journalism seem very milk and water by comparison. The paper really lambasted my move. A leader in June 1910 was scathing: "The *Horse and Hound*, always well informed, published a statement in its last issue that there was a movement on foot for the formation of a union of lads engaged in racing stables. For this promised blessing owners, and trainers in particular, are indebted to a gentleman — who has the honour to claim the modern-novelish name of Mr. J. Fairfax-Blakeborough — described as a Northern sporting writer. It is perhaps to be regretted that Mr. J. Fairfax-Blakeborough does not confine his time to sporting literary efforts, for no matter what their merit might be, they would be preferable to his meddling in affairs that are already in abler and more experienced hands. Might it be suggested, being a northern sports writer, that he turns his attention to work on, say, 'How Dr. Cook reached the North Pole' instead of attempting to force his presence among a community that has no use for him?

"It is proposed by this Northern sporting writer to start an agency, with presumably a paid secretaryship and a few other stipendiary billets attached (1) to supply trainers with suitable lads (2) to protect the interests of those lads and somewhat improve their condition and moral tone. Is it to be assumed that the present system of binding a trainer not to engage a stable servant without first obtaining a reference from his previous employer is harsh and unreasonable? Even though the stable servant has the common right as laid down by the Rules of Racing to appeal to the Stewards of the Jockey Club? Or is it asserted by Mr. J. Fairfax-Blakeborough that the Stewards of the Jockey Club, though independently having the interests of both lads and employers at heart are incapable?

"Whatever may be this estimable gentleman's ideas as to the moral tone of the stable lads and what salary he might ask if he gave himself the post of secretary in the event of such a union being formed, he can rest assured that both owners and trainers, not omitting the public, are justly contented that the Stewards of the Jockey Club shall remain guardians of the lads in racing stables without alien interference.

"Trades Unions have been the curse of the country and it is unlikely that sportsmen, who of all men are just and generous, will consent to adopt a policy which has so often proved suicidal to all concerned. The announcement goes on to say that this proposed agency will be prepared 'to act between stable servants and trainers in cases of dispute, which sometime ago on the Continent was likely to stop racing.' Assuming this to be correct, the situation was brought about by those incendiaries, the paid servant of the Union who had never ridden in a race or strapped a horse in their lives. Such servants must do something for their money, and a strike or threatened strike is the only show they can put up. But it is a falsehood, nothing else, to state that racing in France was likely to be stopped by a few malcontents being incited to rebellion at Maisons-Lafitte. No such apprehensions existed across the Channel, though it was much exaggerated by the Press on this side. There is nothing to be gained, and by no reason to be found for a Union of stable lads to be formed in England. They receive fair wages, their interests are cared for by the rulers of the Turf, who control the Bentinck Benevolent Fund, and who in cases of distress extend this charity to them, their widows and their children. A well behaved lad need never be out of a good situation, in fact, there are not enough to supply the demand. Hence this innovation of Mr. J. Fairfax-Blakeborough is unnecessary and it is to be trusted will prove futile."

This attack was outrageous. To suggest that I was trying to make a highly paid job for myself was a disgraceful way of clouding the real issue which was the way in which stable staff were being treated in those days. My thoughts were for them and only them — and I certainly did not want to play part in the formation of a socialist style trades union. Anyway the following week *The Winning Post* carried this paragraph: "Union of Stable Lads — Mr. J. Fairfax-Blakeborough has sent us a long reply to the article which appeared in these columns under the above heading, and we regret that its length prevents our publishing it in its entirety. We wish to do every justice to Mr. Fairfax-Blakeborough and if, as he thinks, anyone of our readers also imagined that we attacked him, we at once state this was not our desire at all. What we condemned was the idea of a Union of Stable Lads being formed and this we repeat with firmness. As to Mr. Fairfax-Blakeborough, apart from this one matter, we have nothing to say except in praise of him. He was once a contributor to *The Winning Post*, and is a sportsman. If in our endeavour to crush what we believed to be a likely evil we said anything to hurt the feelings of our friend, we much regret it."

I also received a letter from the paper's owner, Bob Sievier, from the Bedford Hotel, Brighton: "Dear Mr. Blakeborough: Your letter has been forwarded to me. I am sorry you have written such a lengthy reply as they tell me at the office they are cramped for space this week so I have instructed them that notice must be taken of the exceptions you take to the leader you refer to. I am sorry if you have taken the remarks to heart but it is obvious I believe, that a Union such as was suggested would only be mischievous."

Obviously this did not help my cause at all. My idea of an association to help all stable staff was doomed. Many had to depend on charity from the Jockey Club for another 60 years. Now my "innovation" is here. But 60 years ago the Jockey Club was dead against it, too. I contacted several members seeking their support, among them the 17th Earl of Derby, a Jockey Club Steward and grandfather of the present Earl. In a letter from Derby House, Stratford Place, London, dated July 25, 1910, Lord Derby replied: "I naturally appreciate efforts that may be made to improve the lot of anybody associated with the sport of racing, but I honestly cannot give any support to your proposal. I think that the attempt to form a union is impolitic, and to a certain extent impracticable. It would lead to endless trouble and in some respects would come into contact with the rules of the Jockey Club. I am afraid therefore that far from supporting your scheme I must honestly declare myself a strong opponent, and I am afraid that you will find my position is the one that will be taken by the vast majority of racehorse owners. The matter has not been undiscussed by members of the Jockey Club, and I think that you may take it from me that there would be opposition on their part to any such proposal as you make."

I persevered for a time but the reaction from other Jockey Club members and owners was just as Lord Derby predicted. The Racing Top Table saw to it that my scheme never got off the ground, so surely missing a sensible opportunity to protect and educate essential stable staff. The lads had to wait more than half-a-century before getting the backing of a specific organisation to help them with their problems, and the establishment of an official "school" to educate them in the arts of horsemanship and basic stable management techniques.

Yet the 17th Earl of Derby played some part in negotations that led to the giant Transport and General Workers Union becoming representative of some stable lads in the late 1930s. The Stable Lads' Association — more akin to the organisation that I sought — was formed during recent months and both the S.L.A. and T.G.W.U. are represented on the Joint Council for Stable Staff. The Jockey Club and the rest of the racing world have caught up with my 1910 ideas but, surely, too late for any association to be non-political and aimed solely for the benefit of the Turf in general. My "union" would have cured some serious Turf ills long before they festered.

I have also lived to see the Jockey Club appoint a regular staff who supervise racemeetings. The National Association of Bookmakers and these officials have ensured that the gangs which used to infest courses have been totally wiped out.

I am particularly proud to have played an important part in guaranteeing that Justice is now more clearly seen to be done when "offenders" are summoned before the Jockey Club. By championing the cause of Jim Adams and others, I have made it quite impossible for "conviction by letter" and these days sentences are usually for a prescribed period. This must be to the benefit of all.

On the credit side, too, I have made many friends. I find people on the Turf the most genuine, generous and interesting. I much prefer National Hunt Racing, to the Flat. I always think that there is more real sport and less commercialism at jumping fixtures. There is more true sportsmanship, too, even today when the whole character of racing under both codes has altered dramatically. A John Porter or William I'Anson reincarnated would barely recognise the sport of today.

Naturally all these changes have had their effect on the character and atmosphere of the Turf. Maybe it is the prejudice of an old and conservative man, or the dimmed vision of a veteran still lingering on a stage from which his favourite actors have departed, but I am inclined to think that the true sporting leaven of old times has disappeared, too. With it has gone much of the friendliness and brotherhood which made the paddocks so pleasant. Certainly the leisurely, open-air club aspect of racing is lacking. The Turf is now much more of a business. There is greater bureaucratic control, regimentation and hustle and this has inevitably destroyed much of what was so charming years ago.

There is no denying the fact that having become a business, the conduct of racing today is much better than it was under the old regime. Whether it is more enjoyable and as sound at core from a sporting standpoint, is another matter.

Personally I should have hated to have had the photo-finish as an ally when I was judging. When the camera was first introduced, Lord Hamilton of Dalzell said to me that he thought the money spent on installing photo-finish cameras on racecourses could have been much better employed in other ways. He added "There is very little wrong with our judges or judging."

Nevertheless, the public seems to like the camera to be

used officially and the Jockey Club insisted on meetings installing it whether they want it or not. This, together with the enormously increased overhead charges due to the army of new officials, was very hard on some struggling little meetings. They have now to pay for Stipendiary Stewards (known as Stewards' secretaries), veterinary surgeons, shorthand writers, and other Jockey Club officials, all posts created during the last decades.

At the latter end of his time as clerk of the course at Wetherby, my old friend the late Henry Crossley, told me that it cost the executive more in payments to police than was required in his early days to run the whole meeting, stakes included.

For over 70 years, I have played the sporting game pretty well all round. For me sport is a form of recreation in the pursuit of which men and women are aided by either horses and hound, or both. That, however, is a debateable point for football, cricket and even motor-cycle racing enthusiasts, all claim to be sportsmen and to be taking part in sport. In the main, however, my own interest have been centred in those outdoor pursuits in which horse and hound play an essential part.

"God gave us memory that we might have June roses in December." I can still vividly recall local sport and sportsmen of 70 years ago. It is a pleasure to bring back the fragrance of these June roses into the December of my life.

Horses have always been the dominating factor in my life. At the age of four the heritage of my Fairfax ancestors asserted itself when I saw two distant kinsmen in the splendour of Yorkshire Hussar uniform, mounted on home-bred Cleveland Bays. So impressed was I that I can recall being transfixed with admiration of what, in my imagination, was the equivalent of two field-marshals riding Turf triple crown winners. From that moment, I decided that horses, riding and cavalry were to be my life. I have never lost my interest in and affection for the Cleveland Bay breed, which was fixed in type anterior to the

Thoroughbred — founded from the same Yorkshire racing galloways as the Cleveland Bay.

All but five of the *General Stud Book* listed 70 some mares from which every thoroughbred in the world descends were located in Yorkshire. The Cleveland Bay contains some of the blood of the Darley Arabian and the best of the early Thoroughbred sires. I was for years Hon. Secretary and latterly President of the Cleveland Bay Horse Society and have lived to see the breed used by almost every country in the world, not only to draw the stage coaches of kings and rajahs, but also to upgrade native breeds. The fact that they are making such high prices in the horse market and that the Bay is now recognised as one of the best foundations for breeding hunters and event horses, and Her Majesty's affection and patronage of the Society, gives me great satisfaction. The nature of the Cleveland Bay and the evolution of the breed is most interesting. Cleveland Bays were first used as pack horses, then as general utility animals in agriculture, then as coach and carriage horses and, with a cross of blood, bold weight-carrying hunters. One such cross was placed long ago in the Grand National. Cleveland Bays were my first horse love and remain so with the Thoroughbred competing in a photo finish.

I have seen the thoroughbred change considerably during my years on the Turf — not all the changes are for the better, either. A far tougher breed of horses raced when I was young. Then "good" horses were not wrapped in cotton wool, and the accent was on staying ability and not speed. When I started racing, the older sportsmen told me about their youth when almost all racehorses were able to stay four miles. Now, of course, the Derby (12 furlongs) is the race that owners throughout the world want to win. The St Leger (14 furlongs) is sadly far less popular with each successive season, while the rich spring handicaps increase in popularity with a public obsessed with gambling. Not until the last quarter of the 18th century did two-year-old racing come into general practice, but today these youngsters command most attention, while during the winter months hurdle races appear more generally popular than steeplechases.

Britain lost a tremendous number of good blood horses, hunters and riding horses during the First World War. I was an unhappy eye-witness of the execution of many hundreds of these. The loss must have had a very seriously adverse affect on the breeding of good stayers on the Flat, over hurdles and fences. The death toll in France was indeed serious. And since 1918 horses have continued to cross the Channel to the sad depletion of British blood lines. Between 1918 and 1952 some 46 stallions and 1,500 mares were sold into French racing stables. Nearly 200 of these mares proved either dams of grandams of "classic" winners. Since 1952 the drain has, if anything, increased with good British blood horses being exported to Japan, America, South America — every corner of the Globe.

Nowadays I can no longer ride to hounds and rarely go racing. When I do go racing I find that I have outlived my generation. There are few breeders, owners and trainers I know now and some of the young men who own studs, or train and ride are apt to consider have-beens like myself as out-dated, out-moded and rather a bore. Eventually they will realise that there is much truth in the old saying: "There is nothing which can make a bigger fool of a man than women and horses."

Although the total betting turnover on racecourses is certainly greater today than when I commenced racing there are not the heavy gamblers there used to be in my early days. There were many men who regularly bet in thousands, who could not think in less than hundreds, but the "break the ring" type is extinct. They would lose £10,000 or £20,000 in a day on the course, and either win it back or lose as much again at the card-table at night. They nearly all came to the same end — drawing from the well until it was dry.

There were in my youth lots of men who regularly bet in "monkeys" or thousands, and had their bets taken by the rails bookmakers like William Hill who did not blink an eyelid at laying the odds to such amounts. It would not be possible today to find bookmakers who would accommodate them.

Most gamblers of birth and position paid their debts of honour although it meant parting with all they had. There were others, however, who drew from bookmakers when they won and "knocked" for a huge amount at the finish. More than one old-time bookmaker told me that he would have been a wealthy man if he had been paid all that was owing to him.

Jim Broadbent, who was over 90 years old when he died, recalled how, when he worked the commissions for some of the leading stables, he often had thousands to get on when the odds were most favourable; and with such rapidity that the bulk of the commission was booked before the sudden influx had time to bring down the price. He had to beat the tic-tac men eager to impart warning news in their own remarkable and effective way. Broadbent continued to act — almost up to his death — as commissioner for stables, but the amounts he was instructed to lay out were not a tenth of those regularly risked at the commencement of this century. There are occasional big coups brought off, but these are from a comparatively small outlay, and though we hear of the successes, the failure of carefully engineered schemes never reaches the headlines.

There were a lot of little meetings, now dead, in the North at which I used to run racehorses. One was Hedon, near Hull — which fell into abeyance but at whose revival I attended in 1901. I saw the end of racing at Scarborough in 1907, at Malton three years before that, and was also at the final meetings at Blackpool, Grindon (near Sunderland), Brocklesby, Rotherham, Shincliffe and Picton. At these defunct courses — with the exception of Blackpool, which offered big stake money but had a short existence — there were only £40 or £50 races. But in those days I think we raced more for the fun of the thing, and for the joy of meeting kindred spirits, than is the case in these more commercial times. Often we had to find our own stabling and pay for it. There was no travelling allowance, free lunch tickets, nor complimentary badges for clubs, and no taking friends in free. Today demands from owners increase annually. Of course their racing costs them a great deal more with rocketing bloodstock prices, trainer's fees and expenses.

There was no more racing at Shincliffe after May 6, 1914, when Capt. Rogerson, Col. Vaux and Col. Roly Milvain were stewards. The meeting had been started in 1895 by Capt. Rogerson, long Master of the North Durham Hunt. A brother of George Menzies was the first clerk of the course. He lived nearby at Coxhoe as did George, who trained a lot of winners there. His nephew Sid Menzies, who later trained at Broughton, near Stokesley, started to ride for Uncle George when he was still a schoolboy. He became one of the leading North country steeplechase jockeys.

Menzies had Joe Kay and Dicky Wilkinson as steeplechase and flat race jockeys respectively. Kay died at Richmond and Wilkinson at Middlesbrough, where, I believe, he was cellarman at a Middlesbrough pub — the most unsuitable job, I should have thought, he could possibly have had. Had it not been for the bottle Dicky Wilkinson would have gone to the top of the tree as a jockey. Like Cornelius Foy, he was given more than one chance to pull himself together, but it was no good. Always at Stockton race times when I was living at Norton, I had calls from Foy, Kay and Wilkinson, who had their round of racing men they knew would remember old and happier times and put their hands in their pockets. An uncle of Sid Menzies told me that almost the last words Sid spoke was a message he sent me thanking me for some little acts of kindness.

Richard Ord, who lived at Sands Hall, owned the Sedgefield course. He was secretary of the South Durham Hunt for years and after that was appointed a handicapper. Almost from the outset he had as his assistant, Jack Dennis of Bishop Auckland, who succeeded him and became one of the best handicappers we have ever had in this country. I knew him from the days when he was little more than a boy and used to see him when visiting Ord at Sands Hall.

I first attended a Thirsk race meeting in the spring of 1902. Recently I took down from my library shelves *The Racing Calendar* for 1902. It makes me feel very much a museum piece. There is not a single owner, trainer, jockey or race official still alive who played a part at that Thirsk fixture. Lots of the jockeys who were riding on that spring day have names entirely unknown to me and so conjure up no past memories. Several others I later got to know intimately.

One was Johnny McCall, son of the Dunbar trainer. He was quite useful but never so good as his brother, George, who made quite a name for himself. To the end of George's career he had a boy's weight with a man's head and strength. I always considered him one of the best jockeys of his day. In 1931, the year after he had given up riding, he came into the weighing room at Hamilton Park to have a word with me and I jokingly said "I'll weigh you out, George, for old times' sake." He got into the scale and registered 7st 11lb, the weight he was when he relinquished his licence.

George rode a lot for Col. McCalmont, Col. Hall Walker — afterwards Lord Wavertree — the Rothschild stable and Frank Hartigan. I remember him once going through the card at Beverley, though one race ended in a dead-heat. At the latter end of his time he occasionally rode out for John Boyd, who followed John McCall at Westbarns, Dunbar. George died in 1948.

John McCall, jnr, I fancy, ended his days a year or two ago in Penrith, where for some years he had acted as boots at the George Hotel, long the property of the Armstrong family. At the 1902 Thirsk meeting to which I am referring John rode a winner, beating William Elsey's remarkable mare Xenie. She was ridden by Yarnell, who for some years had most of Elsey's riding. I recollect that after Xenie had been at stud for a year or two she was brought back into training, and won races, more than once competing against her own daughters.

Walter Sanderson was another who rode a winner at the Thirsk meeting. Seth Chandley was getting a bit long in the tooth in 1902 but went on riding for a year or so longer for Dobson Peacock's Middleham stable. Jim Fagan had a ride in practically every race.

Little Tommy Weldon was another old-timer riding at the Thirsk 1902 meeting. He was born at Beverley and latterly trained there after selling Tupgill, Middleham to Bob Armstrong. Fred Osborne had one or two mounts for his famous father's stable. Fred had not inherited his father's skill, and always seemed to be suffering from a feeling of inferiority.

I am often asked if I consider the jockeys of today as clever as those riding when I was young. My opinion is that they are quite as clever but many of them are not such good horsemen in the true sense of that term. During the last 30 or 40 years we have had a better educated and brainier type of lad apprenticed. Brains count for a lot in race riding, as do ability to judge pace, to be able to estimate how much more the horse can give and how much the most feared opponents have left. I think our leading jockeys of today can give a more intelligent account of both how their own mount and other horses in a race have run than could some of the past generation. John Osborne knew the importance of this ability, but he was an exception.

Another noticeable thing about the jockeys of half a century ago and those of today is that the latter are much more level-headed. Success no longer makes them so cocky and impudent and suddenly finding themselves with money to burn no longer results in them throwing it away as did jockeys like Tiny Heppell, Cornelius Foy, Dick Wilkinson, Chandley and several others I could mention.

Another question frequently put to me is: "What changes in stable management at training quarters have you noticed since

1900?" The three which have most struck me are as follows:

Firstly, the less vigorous strapping of horses, the reduced time spent in muscling-up both racehorses with wisp and rubber, and the increasing use of mechanical coat cleaners. It may not be that trainers and stud grooms value strapping less, but rather that we have lost the mould of the old-time stablemen and that today they have more horses to look after. Jim Adams insisted on lads taking off their coats and waistcoats and spending at least an hour in dressing their horses, putting all their strength behind wisps and rubbers. Time out of count I heard him say — while he watched with eagle eye and finally inspected the coat of every horse — "love your horses, but strap them as though you hated them." His theory was: "An extra ten minutes with a wisp is better than an extra feed of corn."

Secondly, the dress of grooms and lads in racing stables. Look at any photograph of the staffs of either taken before the Second World War and it will be seen they all wore well-fitting riding breeches and leather leggings. All were neat and looked the part. Today they wear slacks pushed into gum boots, and not over-clean jerseys. They seem to have no sartorial pride, or concern for the reputation of those who employ them. Some of the lads leading horses round the parade ring at race meetings are long-haired, uncouth scallywags. What a difference to the time when those in racing and hunting stables wore the livery of their master, plus crested buttons and top hat.

Thirdly, the evolution in feeding horses and the enormous rise in cost of all horse fodder and tack. The now-common use of cubes is a partial return to methods in vogue three hundred years ago when "horse bread" was commonly fed. One finds evidence of this in the records of Beverley Corporation, the centre of an area which was famed for its studs, its Turf associations, its packs of hounds and its sportsmen. In 1458 a bye-law was passed that "no other shall bake horse bread, but shall buy it from common bakers. Penalty ¾d." As to hay, a veteran ex-trainer said to me recently, "they don't seem to be so nearly particular about hay now as we used to be. If I was still at the game I would never buy baled hay, and I wouldn't have a long-haired lad about the place."

In my youth, there was quite a ritual before hay was given to thoroughbreds. It was well shaken and then damped to avoid any dust which might affect the lungs of the horses. As much care was taken in finding high-class land hay as there was in selecting fat short oats, and putting these through a hand-manipulated crusher to avoid them passing whole without benefit to horses. Now some trainers argue that by shaking hay, the seeds with their feed value are lost.

From my early days in racing stables, I was taught the value of an occasional green feed for horses and in my cavalry days I caused raised eyebrows when I ordered the men in my troop to bring a handful of dandelions to evening stables to give to their horses with their evening feed. There was some ridicule as to what were called "Fairfax salads" but they certainly proved worthwhile. Dandelions and boiled beans were part of the manger creed of old trainers in my youth, but are now discounted in favour of the various powders, which may have a stimulating effect but which may also lead to trouble under doping rules.

I am frequently asked too about the changes I have seen in hunt point-to-points and at regular Turf fixtures both on the flat and under National Hunt Rules. So far as the former goes, point-to-points are very different from those I remember and took part in seventy years ago. Then competitors rode over a natural course in hunting or rat-catcher kit. There were few spectators, no racing colours or made fences, no horses were bought as likely point-to-pointers, no women riders, or attempts to make hunt meetings as nearly like regular race fixtures as possible. Now, point-to-points draw big crowds and give essential fillips to Hunt finances. Fences are made and officially inspected and courses are chosen so that there is a hill from which the crowd can have a view of every fence jumped.

As to racing generally at old-established courses, there has been the same kind of change. So far as "amenities" go, there has been much improvement since the days of my youth but The Sport of Kings has altered sadly both in character and paddock atmosphere during my time. It is no longer a leisurely sport valued by horse lovers who provided most of the finance. Of course, old fogeys like myself are too prejudicially bound up with old days and old ways, to appreciate many of the changes which revolutionised racing and we are rather apt to stick our necks out and criticise.

I think the views of Lord Hamilton of Dalzell are in accord with many old-timers as well as my own. After he and Sir Loftus Bates had finished a long discussion during dinner after a Hamilton Park race meeting, he turned to me and said, "I know you don't approve of the Tote, but Sir Loftus and I see that it is going to be essential to the economy of racing in the near future." He was then Senior Steward of the Jockey Club and one of the main organisers of the Tote's introduction. After the remark, he went on with sadness in his voice to look into the future. So impressed was I that I can quote his words almost verbatim even at this space of time. His accurate foresight is interesting and topical today. Here are his words:

"Racing is becoming more and more a commercialised business. We have got to accept this however unpalatable. Will it, before the end of this century, have so eclipsed and strangled the true soul and original objective of those who founded the Turf that it no longer remains a sport? The days are gone when owners were satisfied with winning a £100 or £200 race on the flat and a £50 or £100 steeplechase. Then most men enjoyed the atmosphere of the paddock which was a sort of open air club where one met congenial spirits. We found more pleasure in discussing the make, shape and pedigree of horses in the parade ring, plus watching their performance and that of jockeys, than in the betting ring. No amount of increased prize money can make up for the loss of soul, tradition and true purpose of racing. I have fears for the future of the Turf. We may not live to see it but there is every indication that the destruction of the soul of the sport and the prostituting of racing to the realms of commercialism will so alter its character that the public will ask for no more than an animated roulette board like greyhound racing, plus all manner of extraneous gimmicks." The date of that so accurate prophesy was 1929.

Now that I have retired after 70 years at the racing game, in every facet of which I played a part; I sometimes wonder if it has all been worth while. I made many friends and have helped many newcomers. So, perhaps, mine has not been altogether a wasted life. I like to think I really did engender affection in the hearts of some. Lord Crathorne said that this was so when he handed me the model of a racehorse, made in silver, which was a retirement present given me by owners, trainers, jockeys and racecourse executives. The champagne party which followed in the Catterick Stewards' room was my Turf swan song. If it brought relief it also brought sadness. Perhaps the message on my Christmas card that year reflects and epitomises this: "The end of the year inevitably compels introspection and personal stock-taking. The close of 1961 for me brought to an end what for nearly sixty years has been an integral part of my life. On December 26 I acted as clerk-of-scales for the last time. At Catterick on December 30 I ceased to be a Turf official. A few days later I entered my 80th year. There is not much before one at 80! I can never forget the friends, the hounds, the horses and the racecourses. They all stand out as joyous cameos in my long life."

Since 1962 I have been happy at Low House. I was delighted when I was awarded the O.B.E. in 1975 for my writing and Turf work. Now I spend my days gardening and walking in lovely Westerdale and I am writing still. I have completed four volumes of Turf history detailing the stories of race meetings alive and dead. Stored on my shelves is enough information for another six volumes but time is too short . . . .

INDEX